PRACTICAL
STRESS MANAGEMENT

A Comprehensive Workbook for Managing Change
and Promoting Health

John A. Romas
Mankato State University

Manoj Sharma
The Ohio State University

ALLYN AND BACON

Boston London Toronto Sydney Tokyo Singapore

32169080

8-24-95

Copyright ©1995 by Allyn & Bacon
A Simon & Schuster Company
Needham Heights, Mass. 02194

ISBN 0-205-16301-7

Printed in the United States of America
10 9 8 7 6 5 4 3 2 1   99 98 97 96 95

To Judi and Jennifer
&
Mom and Dad

J.A.R.

To Mummy, Daddy, and Guruji
&
Sulekha, Ankita, and Malvika

M.S.

Contents

List of Illustrations and Tables

Foreword

When invited to write a foreword to a manual or workbook on **Practical Stress Management**, I immediately accepted because of the excitement about how useful a personal workbook on managing stress could be. There was also the conviction that the authors would do a thorough and competent job in carrying out the task. A serious human need would thus be met.

The role of a foreword varies greatly from one book to another while still others get along well without one. In some it becomes an endorsement of the book and/or its authors; in others it functions as an introduction, an overview, or a preface to the document. This one may well be a little of all of these.

That stress is a pervasive presence in Western Culture is more than obvious. The pressure to do one's work faster, thus achieving greater productivity, yet with higher quality is the drumbeat of the production economies of the developed world. These forces have often reached well beyond material production and have invaded every aspect of Western life. Since this "pressure" is far from being the main or only source of stress in our society, it is offered here merely as an example of the pervasiveness of the problem. At the risk of over simplifying the concept it may be said that stress can be seen as the product of real or perceived friction between the individual and his or her environment. Stress arises from the disharmony one feels between the self and all the forces which impinge upon that self. The authors present a much more comprehensive definition of stress but perhaps this will serve for purposes of a foreword.

The concern that so many individuals have in searching for a way or ways to manage or cope with stress provides all the necessary evidence of the need for a workbook such as this. There is a great deal of literature on stress but a "do it yourself" handbook for the individual who recognizes his/her problem and wants to try to address it is truly lacking. That the workbook can also serve as a course of study or a syllabus for professionals who wish to do training in stress management is an additional advantage. Add to the above that "students" in the process, whether seeking self-help or preparing to teach others, take away a comprehensive workbook in the procedures is still another plus.

There are a number of features of the manual or workbook which could be cited for their usefulness or special value, but the worksheets stand out. These guides to self-analysis, situation analysis, and problem delineation are particularly worthy of note. The way they have been selected or devised; the topics, issues or problems they cover, and the developmental or growth process they follow is especially commendable.

One could not conclude a statement such as this without mentioning the qualifications of the authors. Associate Professor John A. Romas did advanced graduate study here at the University of Michigan while developing his research skills. His continuing work in health promotion and stress reduction as researcher and scholar are viewed with pride. Doctor Sharma we know only by his work. His role as research scholar, his medical expertise, work in community health, health promotion and background in Eastern philosophies and stress management have prepared him well to contribute wide to this work.

The authors' backgrounds in both Western and Eastern cultures have equipped them well to produce a unique guide that draws on the philosophical, social and research reservoirs of both to develop this outstanding publication.

Edwin J. McClendon, M.P.H., Ed.D.
Professor Emeritus, Public Health and Health Education
University of Michigan, Ann Arbor. 1994

Preface

"Health promotion is the process of enabling people to increase control over, and to improve, their health. To reach a state of complete physical, mental, and social well-being, an individual or group must be able to identify and to realize aspirations to satisfy needs, and to change or cope with the environment. Health is, therefore, seen as a resource for everyday life, not the objective of living."

- Ottawa Charter for Health Promotion, 1986
First International Conference on Health Promotion

One of the most remarkable developments in the present time has been the interest shown in health promotion by health professionals all over the world. There is a growing trend in health care of shifting emphasis from curative, institutionalized care to promotive, preventive, self-care. It has generally been recognized and accepted that people should exert greater control over their behaviors in order to lead a productive, satisfying, and balanced life. Furthermore, there are numerous rapid advances in technology which have resulted in changes greatly affecting modern life. Inherent in these changes is stress. It is within this context that we address the adverse effects of stress, thereby reducing risk factors which contribute to many stress related diseases. By managing stress constructively and positively we can prevent the adverse effects of disease from occurring and enhance our quality of life.

Human beings, throughout history, have struggled with and managed stress successfully. Like the development of most fields, stress management has become a scientific discipline. The basics of stress management have been derived from the fields of physiology, psychology, medicine, health behavior, health education, philosophy — particularly oriental systems like Yoga, Zen, Rinzai, Sufism, and others. But, besides the scientific component, stress management is also an art, as each individual is a different entity and this difference needs to be dealt with appropriately.

We are presenting to our readers a pragmatic approach to stress management in a "simple" language. Our emphasis is on practicality based upon scientific research and documented techniques. We have provided a workbook format which is reader friendly. Worksheets, Thoughts for Reflection, Stress Management Principles and Summary Points are provided in each chapter. This approach is not just a compilation of techniques, but has been practically tested in the field, backed by scientific evidence, and is complete and holistic. The workbook is an unique blend of thoughts — contemporary and old, Eastern and Western, medical and behavioral, traditional and scientific. It is geared toward changing our routine thought and behavior patterns and replacing those patterns with practical, action oriented, healthy thinking patterns to manage stress more effectively. We believe that after reading and practicing the methods described in this workbook, the reader will be able to lead a balanced, peaceful, and satisfying life. We are sure that the reader can also introduce this approach to others. This can "trigger" a chain reaction which can help society achieve balance, harmony, and peace. In academic settings this workbook shall be useful as a supplemental text for students in health science, health promotion/health education, preventive medicine, psychology, management, and allied health professions.

We present this workbook to all those who worry — some worry over yesterday — for what they could not do, what mistakes they committed, and what caused them aches and pains. Others worry over tomorrow — for what they will do, what adversities they will face, and what blunders they will commit. But, certainly, it is no use to worry over yesterday because it is not with us anymore, never to return again. And tomorrow has not yet come and may hold innumerable possibilities, but only when the sun rises! Anyone can fight the battle of just one day at a time. It is only when we add the burden of yesterdays and tomorrows that contentment and peace of mind elude us. Therefore, we have to acquire the knowledge, develop skills, and foster a positive attitude to deal with today better. This workbook is an attempt to help us achieve these goals, thereby effectively managing change and promoting health.

We wish to acknowledge all the people who have been instrumental in helping us to develop this workbook, particularly those people, including our students, who have tried, tested, and benefited from the techniques presented during these past years. We are thankful to all our colleagues and reviewers throughout the nation for providing constructive feedback: Barbara A. Brehm Curtis, Smith College; W. Michael Felts, East Carolina University; Allen Pat Kelly, Essex Community College; Frances McGrath-Kovarik, San Jose State University; James F. McKenzie, Ball State University; Glen J. Peterson, Lakewood Community College; Deborah A. Wuest, Ithaca College; and Kathleen J. Zavela, University of Northern Colorado. We are also thankful to Winston W. Benson, Harry Krampf, Harold Slobof, B.L. Sharma, and Sharon Zablotney for their valuable advice at the initiation of this workbook project. We are grateful to Kevin Stone, Laura Pearson, and Suzy Spivey, Editors from Allyn and Bacon, our Publishers, for their contributions during the various stages of this Workbook. We would also like to thank Maria P. Szarke, Clinical Dietitian, at Immanuel St. Joseph's Hospital, Mankato, for providing us with updated information on nutrition, and Krystyna M. Romas for providing excellent editorial comments. Finally, we are much obliged to our families for their sacrifice, continued love, and support.

J. A. Romas & M. Sharma

CHAPTER 1

UNDERSTANDING STRESS

The Human Seasons

Four Seasons fill the measure of the year;
There are four seasons in the mind of man:
He has his lusty Spring, when fancy clear
Takes in all beauty with an easy span:

He has his Summer, when luxuriously
Spring's honey'd cud of youthful thought he loves
To ruminate, and by such dreaming high
Is nearest unto heaven: quiet coves

His soul has in its Autumn, when his wings
He furleth close; contented so to look
On mists in idleness - to let fair things
Pass by unheaded as a threshold brook

He has his Winter too of pale misfeature,
Or else he would forego his moral nature.

- John Keats

What Is Stress?

If asked whether or not we have experienced stress in our lives, it is quite likely most of us would respond affirmatively. However, if asked to <u>define stress</u> we may not be able to find appropriate words to express ourselves. Our responses would include words such as:

- pressure
- being "down"
- anger
- anxiety
- nervousness
- having "butterflies in the stomach"
- strain
- negative stimulation
- being "uptight"
- depressed

- being "under the weather"
- tension
- being "upset"

It is certainly true that the above terms convey a meaning of stress. However, in order to comprehend stress completely, we need to explore the meaning of stress in depth. Before we proceed any further, let us review our knowledge, attitudes and coping skills pertaining to stress with the help of Worksheets 1.1, 1.2 and 1.3.

Worksheet 1.1
What Do We Know about Stress

We all have some knowledge about stress. However, much of what we know about stress is based on intuition. We have opinions, beliefs, biases, hunches, and misinformation on the basis of which we perceive stress. The following ten questions are designed to provide us with some feedback regarding what we know about stress. Let us read each statement and mark T (True) or F (False).

____ 1. One major stressful event like death of someone close is much more important in causing ill effects of stress than small everyday hassles.

____ 2. Stressors will always precipitate stress.

____ 3. Stress decreases the amount of saliva in the mouth resulting in a feeling of cotton mouth.

____ 4. During stress, energy is conserved.

____ 5. People who are not competitive and have no time urgency are not successful in life and have stress.

____ 6. A person who often says no, loses many friends and ends up having stress.

____ 7. Drinking coffee or tea reduces stress.

____ 8. The good thing about smoking is that it relaxes the body and relieves stress.

____ 9. Exercise helps to build the body but robs it of vital energy causing stress.

____ 10. Acquired behaviors for stress cannot be changed.

FEEDBACK ON WORKSHEET 1.1

1. F   Research shows that everyday hassles are even more detrimental to one's health than major life changes (Lazarus, 1984).

2. F   Stressors only have the <u>potential</u> of eliciting stress. The important thing is how we react (Greenberg, 1993; Smith, 1993).

3. T   Stress leads to two basic physiological processes—stimulation of the autonomic nervous system and the endocrine system. One of the manifestations of these physiological effects is dry mouth (Guyton, 1991).

4. F   During stress the sympathetic nervous system is activated resulting in expenditure of energy (Greenberg, 1993; Selye, 1936).

5. F   Research shows that people characterized by excessive competitive drive, aggressiveness, impatience, and a hurrying sense of time urgency (Type A) are more prone to stress than people with Type B personality traits characterized by no free floating hostility, no time urgency and little competitive spirit (Friedman & Rosenman, 1959).

6. F   Expressing oneself and satisfying one's own needs while not hurting others and saying no is assertiveness and helps to reduce stress (Bower & Bower, 1976; Fensterheim & Fensterheim, 1975; Smith, 1975).

7. F   Colas, coffee, tea, and chocolate contain caffeine which is a pseudostressor or a sympathomimetic drug that results in a stress like reaction (Greenberg, 1993; Girdano, Everly, & Dusek, 1993).

8. F   Nicotine found in tobacco is also a sympathomimetic agent (Greenberg, 1993).

9. F   Exercise is good not only for physical health but also for psychological well-being (Greenberg & Pargman, 1989).

10. F   The basis for stress management programs is that by reducing stressful behaviors and increasing healthful behaviors, one can better manage stress in life (Enelow & Henderson, 1975; Kasl & Cobb, 1966; Green & Kreuter, 1991).

* * * * * * * * * * * * * * * *

Worksheet 1.2
How Are Our Stress Coping Skills ?

We all cope with stress in our lives. However, some of us are overwhelmed with it. Likewise, some situations trigger more stress for us than others. The following ten statements are designed to provide us with some feedback regarding our coping skills with regard to stress. Let us read each statement below and rate our skill.

Item	Excellent	Very good	Satisfactory	Poor	Very Poor
1. Ability to relax whenever I want to relax.					
2. Ability to assert myself while communicating.					
3. Ability to keep my anger under control.					
4. Ability to resolve conflicts at work and home.					
5. Ability to manage time effectively.					
6. Ability to exercise regularly.					
7. Ability to cope with anxiety over future events.					
8. Ability to cope with anxiety over past events.					

Worksheet 1.2 How Are Our Stress Coping Skills? (Cont'd)

Item	Excellent	Very good	Satisfactory	Poor	Very Poor
9. Ability to eat a balanced diet.					
10. Ability to set and implement realistic goals in order to accomplish desired objectives in life.					

FEEDBACK ON WORKSHEET 1.2

This worksheet enhances our own understanding of the various coping skills that we possess with respect to managing stress in our lives. The areas in which we do not have adequate skills can be acquired with patient practice. The chapters in this workbook will enable us to identify skills which we need to develop further.

* * * * * * * * * * * * * * *

Worksheet 1.3
What Kind of Attitude Do We Have about Stress?

All of us have some kind of attitude about stress. While some attitudes helpful in coping with stress others are not so helpful. The following ten statements are designed to provide us with some feedback regarding our attitudes about stress. Let us read each of the following state-ments and rate ourselves.

Item	Strongly Agree	Agree	Not Sure	Disagree	Strongly Disagree
1. People with stress are weak-minded.					
2. Stress management programs are never successful.					
3. Stress management programs are successful.					
4. Stress cannot be managed.					
5. There is nothing like "stress."					
6. Other people cause my stress.					

Worksheet 1.3 What Kind of Attitude Do We Have about Stress?   (Cont'd)

Item	Strongly Agree	Agree	Not Sure	Disagree	Strongly Disagree
7. I never experience stress, but other people around me are stressed.					
8. Stress is not harmful.					
9. The more we worry about future happenings, the better we can shape them.					
10. If one sets a goal, makes a plan, and implements the plan, then his/her stress levels can be reduced.					

FEEDBACK ON WORKSHEET 1.3

1. All of us experience stress from time to time and it is not a question of being weak-minded or not.

2-4. Evidence exists that stress management programs are successful in reducing the levels of stress which we experience in our lives. These programs substantially reduce stress and the harmful negative consequences associated with stress.

5. Scientific research demonstrates that all of us experience stress from time to time, the only difference is in how we react to it. Denial leads us nowhere. Prudence lies in accepting reality and finding out the most appropriate way for dealing with stress in our lives.

6. No other person can disturb our peace of mind if we choose not to be disturbed. Therefore, no one else except ourselves can be held responsible for stress.

7. We have to be careful not to project stress. All of us encounter stress in our lives.

8. Stress has been known to be associated (directly and indirectly) with a variety of disorders like hypertension, coronary heart disease, stroke, headaches, bronchial asthma etc. (Greenberg, 1993). Denying that stress is not harmful is a negative attitude which hinders our learning the basics of stress management in our lives.

9. Worrying about the future only adds to our stress and is of no use.

10. Scientific evidence indicates that setting a goal and implementing a plan to achieve it is an effective way to reduce stress.

* * * * * * * * * * * * * *

Modern, Contemporary Concepts of Stress in the West

The word stress has been derived from the Latin word *strictus*, meaning hardship, adversity, or affliction. It later evolved in Middle English to be known as *stresse* and in Old French as *estresse*. It has been used in physical sciences, medical science, psychology and behavioral sciences. Stress has been defined from three perspectives, namely environmental or <u>external</u> to the body, as a mental state of tension or <u>internal,</u> and the body's own <u>physical</u> reaction (Rice, 1992). We shall present this concept of stress as it has evolved in the West from response based to event based, and then to the interactional model.

I. <u>Response Based Concept of Stress</u>

In the Western world, the first attempts at defining stress in psychological and behavioral context originated with the work of a physiologist Walter B. Cannon who defined stress as a "fight or flight" syndrome, i.e. when an organism is stressed, either it responds by fighting with the stressor or running away from it (Cannon, 1932). This concept gained currency with the work of Hans Selye on the **General Adaptation Syndrome** (Selye, 1936, 1974a, 1974b, 1982). While attempting to isolate a new sex hormone in rats, he observed that when injected with ovarian extracts, their adrenal glands (endocrine glands located over the kidneys which pour their secretions directly into the bloodstream) secreted corticoid hormones (a steroid), their thymus and lymph nodes became smaller in size, and they developed stomach ulcers. Later, he found that disparate events like cold, heat, infection, injury, loss of blood, and pain also produced similar responses. He labeled this gamut of responses as the General Adaptation Syndrome (GAS) comprised of the following three phases:

- **Phase 1**. <u>Alarm Reaction</u>: In this phase the organism's "homeostasis" or balance is disrupted. The endocrine glands become active — particularly the adrenal glands (secreting corticosteroids) which supply a ready source of energy to the body. This is accompanied by a shrinkage of lymphatic structures, decrease in blood volume, and ulcers in the stomach.

- **Phase 2**. <u>Stage of Resistance</u>: This phase occurs with continued exposure to the agent which elicited the response. In this stage alarm reaction changes cease and opposite changes occur, such as increase in blood volume. But the adaptation energy continues to get depleted.

- **Phase 3**. <u>Exhaustion</u>: This occurs resulting in permanent damage to the system. If the agent is not removed, depletion of all energy of the organism takes place and death may ensue.

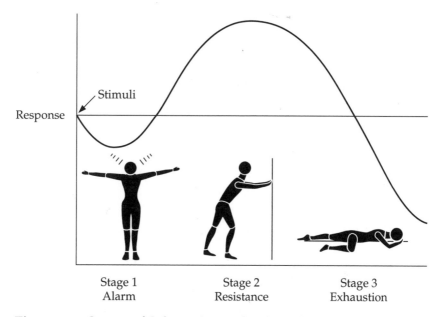

Figure 1-1 Stages of Selye's General Adaptation Syndrome

On this basis, Hans Selye defined stress as "a non-specific response of the body to any demand made upon it" (Selye, 1936, 1964a, 1974b, 1982). Selye, in his later work, found that the same arousal response can be evoked by different situations. Some situations are productive to the organism and this he labeled as **eustress,** while others are harmful and this he labeled as **distress** (Selye, 1982). This was the model of stress based on response and was more physiological in its connotation. The main criticism leveled at this conceptualization has been its neglect of the situational and individual contexts in which stress occurs (Genest & Genest, 1987).

II. Event Based Stress Concept

Thomas Holmes and Richard Rahe (1967) focused on stressful events and constructed a Social Readjustment Rating Scale (SRRS) to assess the amount of stress to which an individual is exposed. The scale developed by Holmes and Rahe (1967) assesses stress by applying weighted life change units to the events in a person's life. These weights are based upon the estimated amount of change or readjustment required for each event on the part of the individual experiencing it. Estimates of this scale have been derived from ratings obtained from a sample of primarily white, middle class adults. The total life stress experienced during a period of time is assessed by summing the weights, or life change units, of the 43 events represented on the Social Readjustment Rating Scale. Before we proceed any further, let us complete Worksheet 1.4 keeping in mind the events which we have experienced during the past one year.

Thoughts for Reflection 1.1

Murphy's Laws

- Nothing is as easy as it looks.

- Everything takes longer than you think.

- If anything can go wrong, it will.

- A day without a crisis is a total loss.

- Inside every large problem is a series of small problems struggling to get out.

- The other line always moves faster.

- Whatever hits the fan will not be evenly distributed.

- No matter how long or hard you shop for an item, after you have bought it, it will be on sale somewhere cheaper.

- Any tool dropped while repairing a car will roll underneath to the exact center.

- You will remember that you forgot to take out the trash when the garbage truck is two doors away.

- Friends come and go, but enemies accumulate.

- The light at the end of the tunnel is the headlamp of an oncoming train.

- The chance of the bread falling with the peanut butter-and-jelly side down is directly proportional to the cost of the carpet.

- The repair man will never have seen a model quite like yours before.

- Beauty is only skin deep, but ugly goes clear to the bone.

Note. Adapted from Murphy's Laws popular in common management parlance.

Worksheet 1.4
The Social Readjustment Rating Scale (SRRS)

Let us focus on the events which we experienced in the past one year. For the events experienced, let us enter the mean value in the score column below.

Rank	Life Event	Mean Value	Score
1	Death of spouse	100	_____
2	Divorce	73	_____
3	Marital separation	65	_____
4	Jail term	63	_____
5	Death of a close family member	63	_____
6	Personal injury or illness	53	_____
7	Marriage	50	_____
8	Fired at work	47	_____
9	Marital reconciliation	45	_____
10	Retirement	45	_____
11	Change in health of family member	44	_____
12	Pregnancy	40	_____
13	Sex difficulties	39	_____
14	Gain of new family member	39	_____
15	Business readjustment	39	_____
16	Change in financial state	38	_____
17	Death of close friend	37	_____

Worksheet 1.4 Social Readjustment Rating Scale (SRRS) (Cont'd)

Rank	Life Event	Mean Value	Score
18	Change to different line of work	36	_____
19	Change in number of arguments with spouse	35	_____
20	Mortgage over $10,000	31	_____
21	Foreclosure of mortgage or loan	30	_____
22	Change in responsibilities at work	29	_____
23	Son or daughter leaving home	29	_____
24	Trouble with in-laws	29	_____
25	Outstanding personal achievement	28	_____
26	Wife beginning or stopping work	26	_____
27	Beginning or ending school	26	_____
28	Change in living conditions	25	_____
29	Revision of personal habits	24	_____
30	Trouble with boss	23	_____
31	Change in work hours or conditions	20	_____
32	Change in residence	20	_____
33	Change in schools	20	_____
34	Change in recreation	19	_____
35	Change in church activities	19	_____
36	Change in social activities	18	_____

Worksheet 1.4 The Social Readjustment Rating Scale (SRRS) (Cont'd)

Rank	Life Event	Mean Value	Score
37	Mortgage or loan less than $10,000	17	_____
38	Change in sleeping habits	16	_____
39	Change in number of family get-togethers	15	_____
40	Change in eating habits	15	_____
41	Vacation	13	_____
42	Christmas	12	_____
43	Minor violations of the law	11	_____
		TOTAL	_____

Note. From The social readjustment scale by T. H. Holmes & R. H. Rahe, Journal of Psychosomatic Research, 11, copyright 1967, Elsevier Science Ltd. Reprinted with permission by Elsevier Science Ltd., Oxford, England.

FEEDBACK ON WORKSHEET 1.4

The total score on this SRRS represents the total life change units experienced by us. The scale assesses stress by applying weighted life change units to the events in a person's life. These weights are based upon the estimated amount of change or readjustment required for each event on the part of the individual experiencing it. These estimates have been derived from a sample of primarily white middle class adults. Therefore, the levels of life change units are subject to modification depending upon social, cultural, and other demographic variables. Furthermore, some of the events, like mortgage, etc. have lost their contemporary significance. But despite these limitations the scale gives a fair amount of idea regarding the stress which we have experienced in the recent past. This view was very popular in the 1970's, and a lot of research substantiated this viewpoint correlating the higher life changes unit scores with illness.
(Holmes & Masuda, 1974; Holmes, 1979; Rahe & Arthur, 1978).

According to this viewpoint, a life change unit score between 150-199 showed a 37 percent chance of these stressors leading to sickness in the following year; scores between 200-299 exhibit a 51 percent chance and scores over 300 a 79 percent chance (Holmes & Rahe, 1967).

* * * * * * * * * * * * * * * * *

During the 1970's the life events concept was very popular. Holmes (1979) estimated that as many as 1000 publications appeared based on SRRS during the 1970's. Some other scales were also developed based on this concept, e.g. Recent Life Changes Questionnaire (RLCQ) (Rahe, 1974), PERI Life Events Scale (Dohrenwend, Krasnoff, Askenasy, & Dohrenwend, 1978). Based upon this concept stressors have been defined as life events or changes which produce or have the potential to produce changes within the individual, family system, and his or her surroundings. However, later work has challenged even this viewpoint. It has been found that stress reactions differ as a function of neurophysiological level of response, qualities of the stressor, and differences among individuals (Genest & Genest, 1987).

III. Interactional Model of Stress

According to this view, which is largely accepted now, the perception of the stressor by the individual is the most important factor. The degree to which anyone is stressed is influenced by a variety of factors. Richard Lazarus (1966, 1984) identified four stages in the process of stress development. The first stage is the primary appraisal of the event. In this stage, based upon previous experiences, knowledge about oneself and knowledge about the event by the individual determines whether he or she is in trouble. If the stressor is perceived to be threatening or has caused harm or loss then the secondary appraisal takes place. If, on the other hand, the event is judged to be irrelevant or poses no threat, then stress does not develop any further. The secondary appraisal essentially constitutes how much control one has over the situation. Based upon this understanding, the individual ascertains what means of control are available to him or her. This is the third stage known as coping. Finally, reappraisal occurs, as to whether the original stressor has been effectively negated or not. These are some of the models prevalent at present which explain the complex phenomenology of stress.

Traditional, Ancient Concepts of Stress in the East

One of the ancient civilizations in the world has been the one which flourished around the Indus valley and later developed into the civilization in South Asia leading to the country which is known to the world today as India. We shall be focusing on the concepts drawn from Indian culture and tradition to represent the concept of stress in the East.

The four *Vedas* — the *Rig,* the *Sama,* the *Yajur,* and the *Atharva* — containing over a hundred thousand verses of ancient seers and sages, form the basis of the philosophy from the East. They are supported by the *Upanishads* — 108 of which have been preserved. Then there are the 18 Puranas, including *Srimad Bhagvatam,* the *Brahma Sutras,* which contain Vedic philosophy in the form of aphorisms, *Yogasutras* of Patanjali, *Tantaras* dealing with esoteric aspects of the spiritual quest, *Manusmriti* containing the codes of conduct, and *Bhagvad Gita,* the gist of Vedas (Singh, 1983). In addition, the *Charaka Samhita* and *Susruta Samhita* were the texts of the Ayurvedic (Indian) system of medicine.

Description of stress is depicted by use of terms like *dukha* (meaning pain, misery or suffering), *klesa* (afflictions), *kama* or *trisna* (desires), *atman* and *ahankara* (self and ego), *adhi* (mental aberrations), and *prajanparadha* (failure of lapse of consciousness) (Pestonjee, 1992).   These varied depictions indicate the holistic dimension of stress in Eastern thought. Pestonjee (1992) notes that according to the Samkhya-yoga system the cause of stress is *avidya* or faulty reality testing of either or all of the following:

- *asmita* (self appraisal)

- *raga* (object appraisal)

- *dvesha* (threat appraisal)

- *abhnivesha* (coping orientation)

According to the Eastern viewpoint, life situations leading to stress can be one of three kinds:

(1) *adhyatmik* (personal) consisting of pathological diseases or psychological afflictions like jealousy, fear, anger, lust, hatred, greed, grandiosity and depression.

(2) *adhibhotik* (situational) consisting of conflicts, competition, aggression, act of war, and so on.

(3) *adhidevik* (environmental) due to natural calamities like earthquake, extremes of temperature, eruption of volcanoes, and so on.

Stress operates through four levels of stressors:

(1) *Prosupta* (Dormant stressors): Any mental process is potentially stressful and can become stressful just like any seed has the potential to germinate into a sapling. For example, a student might imagine that he or she is going to be severely reprimanded if he or she is late for class. This imagination would be a dormant stressor.

(2) *Tonu* (Tenuous or weak stressors): Stressors of insufficient intensity and urgency which are kept under check by more powerful stressors. For example, when one is hungry, the hunger response (powerful stressor) would override worrying about being late for class (tenuous or weak stressor).

(3) *Vichchinna* (Intercepted stressors): These stressors are alternating between stages of dormancy and manifestation. For example, a student who is reprimanded for coming late to class subsequently tries to come on time. The student has a stressor which will manifest when he or she becomes late. This is an intercepted stressor.

(4) *Udara* (Operative stressors): These are stressors which have found complete expression in behavior. For example, a student who has conditioned his or her behavior to be present before time for class is exhibiting this behavior because of an operative stressor.

Hence, Eastern thought primarily places emphasis on the powers of the individual in coping with stress. The individual can, with the help of *vidya* or *gyana* (knowledge and correct perception), understand the situation correctly, with adequate practice *(sadhana)* apply appropriate skills to reduce undue response to stressors and ultimately develop a wholesome attitude devoid of manifest stress *(samadhi bhavana)*. This, in simple terms, is an explanation of the Eastern concept of stress which places an emphasis on the "correct perception" of any event by an individual in dealing with stress.

Effects of Stress on the Body

Another aspect in understanding the concept of stress is the effect which stress has on the body. In this workbook we shall be focusing on a combination of Western and Eastern thought and methodology in the management of stress. Therefore, we have tried to establish a model of stress which imbibes both these viewpoints and is generally well accepted. This has been depicted in Figure 1.2.

Various life situations from the internal or external environment, like loss, problematic relationships, change, poor financial management, sickness and so on affect us. This could be a single event or everyday hassles which accumulate. In the Eastern philosophy stressful life situations have been classified as personal *(adhyatmik)*, situational *(adhibhotik)* or environmental *(adhidevik)*. These life situations are perceived by the cerebral cortex, that is the part of the brain which is responsible for judgement, decision making, and other higher functions. This interpretation is modified based upon our personalities, behavioral styles, values, beliefs, norms and attitudes. Before we proceed any further, let us identify our personality type with the help of Worksheet 1.5.

Figure 1-2 Stress: Development and Intervention

Worksheet 1.5
Personality Type Identification

Let us answer the following questions as either yes or no and count the number of yes responses when completed.

1. Do we accentuate key words in speech and hurry the last few words in our sentences?

2. Do we always eat, walk, talk, and move rapidly?

3. Do we get impatient and irritated when things do not move fast?

4. Do we often attempt to do or think more than one thing at a time?

5. Do we always try to move the topic of conversation to our interest?

6. Do we have feelings of guilt when we relax?

7. Do we frequently fail to take note of new things around us?

8. Are we more concerned with getting things worth having rather than becoming what is worth being?

9. Do we suffer from a chronic sense of time urgency?

10. Do we compete or feel compelled to challenge others?

11. Do we engage in expressive gestures like pounding the table, etc. in conversation?

12. Do we believe our fast pace is necessary?

13. Do we rate life's success in terms of "numbers?"

Note. Adapted from Type A behavior and your heart (p. 100-102) by M. Friedman and R.H. Rosenman, 1974, New York, NY: Fawcett Crest. Copyright 1974 by Meyer Friedman. Adapted by permission from Alfred A. Knopf Inc.

FEEDBACK ON WORKSHEET 1.5

If the total number of our yes responses is more than 7, then we are more likely to be Type A in our orientation. The higher our score is from 7 toward 13, the stronger is the likelihood of your being Type A in our orientation. Type A personality types exhibit excessive competitive drive, are aggressive, impatient, and always have an urgency of time. The basis of this personality is believed to be a free floating form of generalized hostility and a sense of insecurity. If, on the other hand, we have lower scores, we are likely to be Type B in our orientation. Type B personality types, on the contrary, do not have an urgency of time, are not competitive, rather tend to be cooperative and patient. These are the "happy-go-lucky" kind of people.

Type A personality types have been shown to be more prone to stress and its negative consequences. However, these personality type classifications are not rigid assessments and are more situational in their connotation. Importantly, they can be modified.

* * * * * * * * * * * * * * *

The way we behave in day-to-day life constitutes our behavioral style. This aspect has been discussed in greater detail in Chapter 4. According to Eastern philosophy, perception is dependent upon reasoning by self (faulty or correct) and the stage of a stressor-dormant *(prosupta)*, tenuous *(tonu)*, intercepted *(vichchinna)*, or operative *(udara)*

After perception the next stage in the development of stress is the <u>emotional response</u> which triggers the activity in the limbic system. The limbic system is the primitive part of the brain which is the seat of various emotions like anger, fear, insecurity, worry and so on. The negative emotional responses described in Eastern philosophy are *kama* (immoral sexual passion), *krodh* (anger), *madh* (superiority or inferiority complex), *moh* (uncontrolled desires), and *lobh* (greed). The emotional arousal activates the <u>physiological response</u> which is manifested in the form of stimulation of the endocrine glands and the autonomic nervous system. The <u>endocrine glands</u> are the glands which pour their secretions directly into the blood stream. These secretions are called hormones. Hormones are essential chemicals which have a wide range of effects on the body. They need to be produced in optimum amounts in order for the body to function normally. An excess or lack of these vital substances can lead to a variety of pathological disorders. The <u>autonomic nervous system</u> is that part of the central nervous system (brain and spinal cord) which regulates the functioning of vital organs. It consists of the sympathetic and the parasympathetic nervous system. In simplistic terms it can be said that the sympathetic nervous system is the one which is responsible for spending energy, and the parasympathetic nervous system is the one responsible for conserving energy in the body. Figure 1-3 depicts the complex physiological changes which take place in the body as a result of stress.

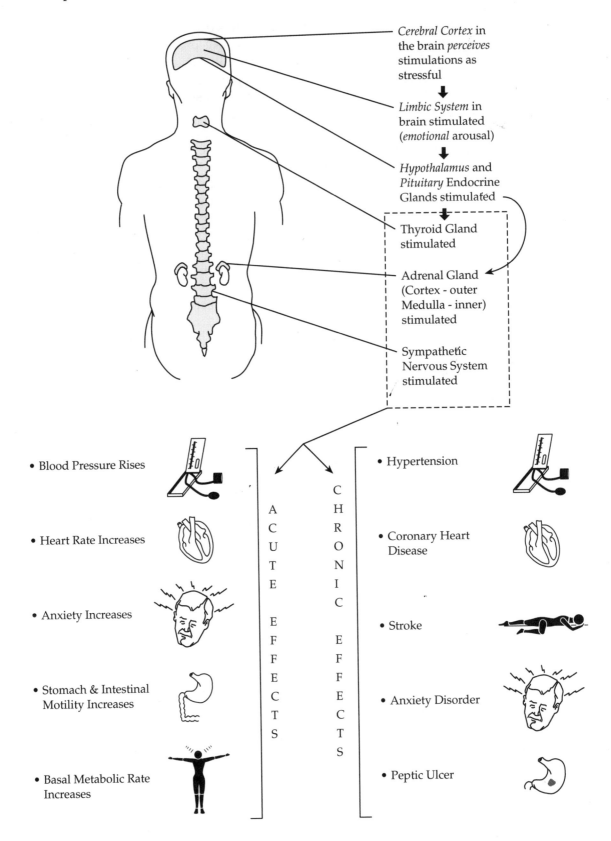

Figure 1-3   Stress Psychophysiology

The net result of both these physiological activities viz. endocrine and autonomic nervous system stimulation is that a variety of chemicals are produced in the body. More often than not these chemical byproducts do not get used and accumulate within the body. These chemical byproducts are responsible for the <u>negative consequences</u> in the body. Stress produces both acute or short-term immediate effects as well as chronic or long term effects. Figure 1-4 presents the various immediate signs and symptoms of acute stress on the human body.

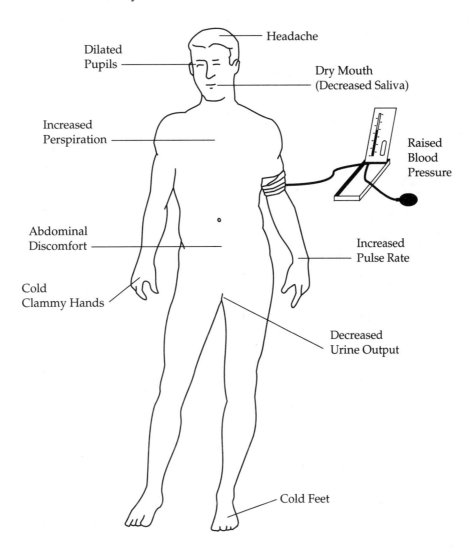

Figure 1-4   Signs and Symptoms of Acute Stress on the Body

Stress, because of its chronic effects, can be a direct causative factor, an indirect contributory factor, a precipitating factor, or an aggravating factor for various diseases. Some of the pathological signs, symptoms and diseases commonly associated with stress are anxiety disorders, insomnia, hypertension, stroke, coronary heart disease, ulcers, migraine headaches, tension headaches, rheumatoid arthritis, temporomandibular joint syndrome, bronchial asthma, and backache (Greenberg, 1993; Rice, 1992).

Stress in the Overall Context

Until now, we have discussed the concept of stress from an Eastern and Western perspective, how it has developed over time, and what the effects of stress are on the human body. This has been more medical, physiological, philosophical, and behavioral in its connotation.   What is also required in this conceptualization is the historical, sociocultural, political, and organizational context in which we experience stress.

From time immemorial, human life has always been ridden with stress.   In premodern times there were greater threats from natural calamities, extremes of temperature, pestilence and so on. In modern times while industrialization has provided many facilities and improvement in the physical quality of life for many of us, these stressors have been replaced by a faster pace of life, rapidly changing technology, divergence in morality, increasing social complexity, and so on. The student of today, the worker of today, the executive of today, and all other people today, have to face greater stress than their counterparts of yesteryear. Woolfolk and Lehrer (1993) note that present society has become individualistic and materialistic in contrast to communal and spiritual society of the past. Never before has a large percentage of the population been without durable and dependable social support in its proper and adequate form. This indeed is a great source of stress.

In the organizational context, which could be work setting, school setting, and/or community setting, stress has been studied quite extensively. Beehr and Newman (1978) have defined job stress in terms of interaction of the person with job related factors which disrupt or enhance his or her psychological and physiological condition.   This organizational stress is further heightened for people in certain specific situations, such as for women who have to accomplish multiple roles and students who are constantly in a phase of transition. In addition, the crisis of the modern human also lies in finding meaning to his or her activities. Often we are unable to attribute meaning and importance to what we are doing in daily life. In the absence of these meaningful activities with coherence and lawfulness, the stress manifestations increase (Antonovsky, 1987; Shepperd and Kashani, 1991). Furthermore, despite all advancements, for a vast majority of people, primarily in the third world, still the basic stress is tied into making two ends meet and mustering enough for food, clothing, and shelter. Therefore, the importance of understanding historical, sociocultural, political, and organizational factors in our lives is also essential for dealing with and managing stress more effectively. Thoughts for Reflection 1.2 helps us reflect upon some of the factors affecting modern life.

Thoughts for Reflection 1.2

Why Stress Exists

Present day life is more complex than ever before. A reflection on some of the factors responsible for this complexity will help us cope with stress better. Following is a list of some of these factors:

- Intricacy of Social Fabric: In personal and work life we have come to a point where our relationships have become extremely complex and challenging. Much of our life revolves around getting into, being in, and getting out of relationships. All these events are potentially stressful.

- Divergence in Morality and Ethics: We have developed a value system which presents us with highly divergent and conflicting standpoints on various aspects of life issues. Adjustments and responses to these contradictions are stressful.

- Conflicting Expectations: Most of the time in our work life as well as our personal life we do not know what is being expected of us. This unclarity about our role is a stressful factor.

- Marginal Communication: Poor and ineffective communication in our day-to-day life is a major source of discomfort and stress in our lives.

- Rapid Change in Technology: The advancement in science and technology has pervaded all walks of life. Inherent in this change is stress.

- Lack of Proper Training to Do What One Is Being Asked to Do: Usually in our work life, owing to the gap between "education" and "profession," we are at times unable to do what is being asked from us. This gap is a strong source of stress.

- Ineffective Management Systems: Despite the innovation and implementation of a wide variety of management systems which have enhanced production and have been responsible for quality products, we have been unable to develop a management system which completely rids us of stress.

- Lack of Job Security: In present times, we do not know if we shall be able to remain in our job or not. This insecurity provides ample stress in our life.

- Limited or no Organizational Loyalty: These days for many of us we cannot associate ourselves with the job which we perform and the organization with which we work. This is an extremely stressful factor.

- Economic Overextension: Pressure which money exerts in all walks of our life is a potent stressor.

* * * * * * * * * * * * * * * *

A comprehensive stress management program needs to address all these contexts and perspectives in order for the program to be successful. It shall be our attempt in this workbook to try to do justice in this regard.

Another aspect which needs to be emphasized is that stress management is essentially a preventive approach. In preventive medicine, prevention occurs at three levels viz. primary, secondary, and tertiary. <u>Primary prevention</u> is the level where the intervention occurs before the disease. In stress management it is the level at the stage of perception of the stressor. <u>Secondary prevention</u> is the level of intervention when the disease process has started. In the case of stress management, it is the stage when emotional arousal and physiological activation has occurred. <u>Tertiary prevention</u> is the level when disease has already caused damage. In the case of stress management, it is the stage when negative consequences have already set in and then we intervene. It is akin to stamping out the fire after the inferno has engulfed the property. In this context it is worth noting that some experts view stress as a risk factor; therefore, stress management, according to them, is primary prevention. However, we would like to view stress as a disease in its developmental form and have, therefore, classified stress management with various levels of prevention described above.

Finally, the importance of one's <u>perception and attitude</u> in comprehending stress and dealing with it cannot be overemphasized. Thoughts for Reflection 1.3 reinforces our belief in the importance of developing a <u>positive attitude</u> which is at the core of all stress management efforts. Stress Management Principle # 1, at the end of this chapter, is also in line with this ideology. It is hoped that the reader will not only memorize this principle, but also try to incorporate it in his or her life.

Thoughts for Reflection 1.3
On Attitude

- Attitude determines our behavior.

- It is up to each one of us as to how we choose to react to any situation.

- What happens to us in life has relatively little effect compared to how we react. If we choose to get upset, worked up, and worried, even a small, trivial event, colored with our imagination, may appear to be devastating. However, if we choose to envision the situation in perspective, and not get upset or worried, then our coping skills are enhanced.

- Effort and directed determination are required for changing attitude.

- Understanding the importance of attitude and its impact upon behavior is more significant than being factual, scientific, and analytical.

Stress Management Principle # 1

**It is not the stressor but the perception
of the stress by us
which is important.**

Summary Points

- Walter Cannon defined stress as a "fight or flight" syndrome, that is, when an organism is stressed either it responds by fighting with the stressor or running away from it.

- Hans Selye described the General Adaptation Syndrome consisting of Alarm Reaction, Stage of Resistance, and Exhaustion. On this basis he defined stress as the "non-specific response of the body to any demand made upon it."

- Thomas Holmes and Richard Rahe constructed the Social Readjustment Rating Scale (SRRS) to assess the amount of stress experienced by an individual due to changing life events.

- Richard Lazarus described stress development in <u>four stages</u> — namely, Primary Appraisal, Secondary Appraisal, Coping, and Reappraisal.

- According to Eastern thought stress is described as *dukha* (pain, misery, suffering), *klesa* (afflictions), *kama* or *trisna* (desires), *atman* and *ahankara* (self and ego), *adhi* (mental aberrations), and *prajanparadha* (failure or lapse of consciousness). The main cause is *avidya* (faulty reality testing).

- Type A personality people (characterized by hurrying nature, competitive zeal, dominating nature, and fast pace of life) are more prone to stress.

- A generally accepted model of stress development consists of life situations which are perceived as stressful, and they lead to emotional and physiological response, thus leading to negative consequences.

- The physiological response in stress basically is comprised of endocrine stimulation and sympathetic nervous system overactivity.

Stress Management Principle # 1 (Cont'd)

- Some pathological signs, symptoms, and diseases associated with stress are anxiety disorders, insomnia, hypertension, stroke, coronary heart disease, ulcers, migraine headaches, tension headaches, rheumatoid arthritis, temporomandibular joint syndrome, bronchial asthma, and backache.

- Stress, besides medical, psychological, behavioral, philosophical contexts, also needs to be understood in sociocultural, political and organizational perspective in order to devise a meaningful stress management effort.

References & Further Readings

Antonovsky, A. (1987). The salutogenic perspective: Toward a new view of health and sickness. Advances, 4, 47–55.

Beer, T. A. & Newman, H.E. (1978). Job stress, employee health and organizational effectiveness: A facet analysis, model and literature review. Personnel Psychology, 31, 665–699.

Bower, S. A. , & Bower, G. H. (1976). Asserting your self. Reading, MA: Addison-Wesley.

Cannon, W. B. (1932). The wisdom of the body. New York, NY: W.W. Norton.

Dohrenwend, B. S., Krasnoff, L., Askenasy, A. R., & Dohrenwend, B. P. (1978). Exemplification of a method for scaling life events: The PERI Life Events Scale. Journal of Health and Social Behavior, 19, 205-229.

Enelow, A. J., & Henderson, J. B. (Eds.) (1975). Applying behavioral science to cardio-vascular risk. New York, NY: American Heart Association.

Fensterheim, H., & Fensterheim, B. (1975). Don't say yes when you want to say no. New York, NY: David McKay.

Friedman, M., & Rosenman, R. H. (1959). Association of specific overt behavior pattern with blood and cardiovascular findings: Blood clotting time, incidence of arcus senilis & clinical coronary artery disease. Journal of American Medical Association, 169, 1286-1296.

Friedman, M., & Rosenman, R.H. (1974). Type A behavior and your heart. New York, NY: Fawcett Crest.

Genest, M., & Genest, S. (1987). Psychology and health. Champaign, IL: Research Press.

Girdano, D. A., Everly, G. S. Jr., & Dusek, D. E. (1993). Controlling stress and tension: A holistic approach. Englewood Cliffs, NJ: Prentice Hall.

Green, L. W., & Kreuter, M. W. (1991). Health promotion planning: An educational and environmental approach. (2nd ed.). Mountain View, CA: Mayfield Publishing Company.

Greenberg, J. S. (1993). Comprehensive stress management. (4th ed.). Dubuque, IA: William C. Brown Publishers.

Greenberg, J. S., & Pargman, D. (1989). Physical fitness: A wellness approach. (2nd ed.). Englewood Cliffs, NJ: Prentice Hall.

References and Further Readings (Cont'd)

Guyton, A. C. (1991). <u>Textbook of medical physiology</u>. (8th ed.). Philadelphia, PA: W. B. Saunders.

Holmes, T. H. (1979). Development and application of a quantitative measure of life change magnitude. In J. E. Barrett, R. M. Rose, & G. L. Klerman (Eds.), <u>Stress and mental disorder</u> (pp.37-53). New York, NY: Raven.

Holmes, T. H., & Masuda, M. (1974). Life change and illness susceptibility. In B. S. Dohrenwend & B. P. Dohrenwend (Eds.), <u>Stressful life events: Their nature and effects</u>. (pp.49-72). New York, NY: Wiley.

Holmes, T. H. & Rahe, R. H. (1967). The social readjustment rating scale. <u>Journal of psychosomatic research</u>, <u>11</u>, 213-218.

Kasl, S. V., & Cobb, S. (1966). Health behavior, illness behavior and sick role behavior. <u>Archives of Environmental Health</u>, <u>12</u>, 246-266.

Lazarus, R. S. (1966). <u>Psychological stress and the coping process</u>. New York, NY: Mc Graw Hill.

Lazarus, R. S. (1984). Puzzles in the study of daily hassles. <u>Journal of Behavioral Medicine</u>, <u>7</u>, 375-389.

Rahe, R. H. (1974). The pathway between subjects' recent life changes and their near future llness reports: Representative results and methodological issues. In B. S. Dohrenwend & B. P. Dohrenwend (Eds.), <u>Stressful life events: Their nature and effects</u>. (pp.73-86). New York, NY: Wiley.

Rahe, R. H., & Arthur, R. J. (1978). Life change and illness studies: Past history and future directions. <u>Journal of Human Stress</u>, <u>4</u>, 3-15.

Rice, P. L. (1992). <u>Stress and Health</u>. (2nd Ed.). Pacific Grove, CA: Brooks/Cole Publishing Company.

Selye, H. (1936). A syndrome produced by diverse nocuous agents, <u>Nature</u>, <u>138</u>, 32.

Selye, H. (1974a). <u>Stress without distress</u>. Philadelphia, PA: Lippincott.

Selye, H. (1974b). <u>The stress of life</u>. New York, NY: Mc Graw Hill.

Selye, H. (1982). History and present status of stress concept. In L. Goldberger & S. Breznitz (Eds.), <u>Handbook of stress: Theoretical & clinical aspects</u>. (pp. 7-17). New York, NY: Free Press.

Shepperd, J. A., & Kashani, J. V. (1991). The relationship of hardiness, gender, and stress to health outcomes in adolescents. <u>Journal of Personality</u>, <u>59</u>, 747-768.

References and Further Readings (Cont'd)

Singh, K. (1983). Hinduism. In <u>Religions of India</u> (pp. 17-74) New Delhi, India: Clarion Books.

Smith, J.C. (1993). <u>Understanding stress and coping</u>. New York, NY: Macmillan Publishing Company.

Smith, M.J. (1975). <u>When I say no, I feel guilty</u>. New York, NY: The Dial Press.

Woolfolk, R. L., & Lehrer, P. M. (1993). The context of stress management. In P. M. Lehrer, & R. L. Woolfolk (Eds.), <u>Principles and practice of stress management</u> (2nd ed.) (pp. 3-14). New York, NY: The Guilford Press.

CHAPTER 2

ENHANCING AWARENESS ABOUT MANAGING STRESS

Infant innocence

Reader, behold! this monster wild
Has gobbled up the infant child.
The infant child is not aware
It has been eaten by the bear.

A. E. Housman

Enhancing Awareness about Managing Stress

In the previous chapter we have focused mainly on developing knowledge about stress. An increase in knowledge alone does not always lead to behavioral change. Knowledge of some kind is essential, but the desired action does not occur until and unless we have a strong cue to trigger the motivation (Green & Kreuter, 1991). Therefore, what is also required along with knowledge is an enhanced awareness. In order for us not to be overcome by stress we need to be aware of its presence, manifestations, and the various methods and techniques for managing stress.

Stress is an everyday occurrence for all of us. However, many of us do not acknowledge that we have stress in our lives, and oftentimes this belief interferes in our coping with stress. Becker (1974) developed the Health Belief Model to explain and predict health behavior in terms of certain belief patterns. This model is based upon the following assumptions about behavior change:

- The person must believe that his or her health is in jeopardy.

- The person must perceive the potential seriousness of the condition.

- The person must believe that benefits stemming from the recommended behavior outweigh the costs and inconvenience.

- There must be a "cue to action" or a precipitating force that makes the person feel the need to take action.

Therefore, it is our attempt in this chapter to make a convincing case for changing our life style patterns to reduce stress. We have already seen in the previous chapter that stress has both acute or short term and chronic or long term manifestations which can be harmful to us.

Acute Manifestations of Stress

We have already seen in Chapter 1 that stress produces a number of immediate manifestations. These occur soon after a stressor has affected our body. We need to find out what these changes are in our body. Let us therefore complete Worksheet 2.1 and find out how our body reacts to acute stress.

Worksheet 2.1
How Our Body Reacts To Acute Stress

Let us imagine ourselves in a stressful situation. When we are feeling anxious or stressed, what do we typically experience? Let us check all the items that apply:

_____ 1.   My heart starts to beat faster and pound harder.

_____ 2.   I cannot control disturbing thoughts from entering my mind.

_____ 3.   My hands become cold and clammy.

_____ 4.   I keep brooding on trivial thoughts over and over again.

_____ 5.   I begin to sweat profusely.

_____ 6.   I lose the power to concentrate and function effectively.

_____ 7.   I develop loose motions, irritable bowel or diarrhea.

_____ 8.   I cannot make decisions and feel horrible.

_____ 9.   I cannot sit still and nervously pace up and down.

_____ 10.   I imagine the worst possible scenario and cannot stop from thinking about that.

_____ 11.   My abdomen begins to hurt.

_____ 12.   I feel the world around me is crashing and I have lost all control.

_____ 13.   I feel restless.

_____ 14.   I imagine horrifying scenes which keep me disturbed for a long time.

_____ 15.   My body gets stiff and I am immobilized.

_____ 16.   I think of leaving everything and just running away.

_____ 17.   I have a feeling of "butterflies" in my stomach.

_____ 18.   I want the situation to end favorably as soon as possible but am not sure.

Worksheet 2.1 How Our Body Reacts To Stress (Cont'd)

_____   19.   I feel tired and exhausted after sometime.

_____   20.   I develop headache.

FEEDBACK ON WORKSHEET 2.1

Let us count the even and odd numbered responses separately.

- Odd Number of responses = _____

- Even number of responses = _____

If we have scored more even number responses than odd then we tend to respond to stress with our <u>mind</u>. This also signifies that we are likely to derive greater relaxation by indulging in the activities of mind like meditation, any interesting hobby and so on. If we have scored more odd number responses, then our <u>body</u> tends to respond more to stress. People who respond to stress by having symptoms in the body generally require systematic physical activity like aerobic exercise, progressive muscle relaxation, and other such techniques. If we have a near equal mixture of even and odd number responses then we respond to stress in a <u>mixed</u> fashion. A combination of mind relaxation and physical activities are likely to benefit us in relieving our stress.

<u>Note</u>. Based upon personal discussions with Peter R. Kovacek , Henry Ford Hospital, Detroit, MI, 1981.

* * * * * * * * * * * * * * *

Chronic Manifestations of Stress

Chronic stress is also harmful to us. Chronic stress can permanently raise our blood pressure levels. This condition is known as hypertension. Hypertension has been identified as a risk factor for coronary heart disease (CHD) and cerebrovascular disease or stroke. The cause for 90 percent of these cases of hypertension is not known and these are labeled as essential hypertension (Donatelle & Davis, 1993; Greenberg & Dintiman, 1993). Figure 2-1 shows how stress is related to hypertension and coronary heart disease.

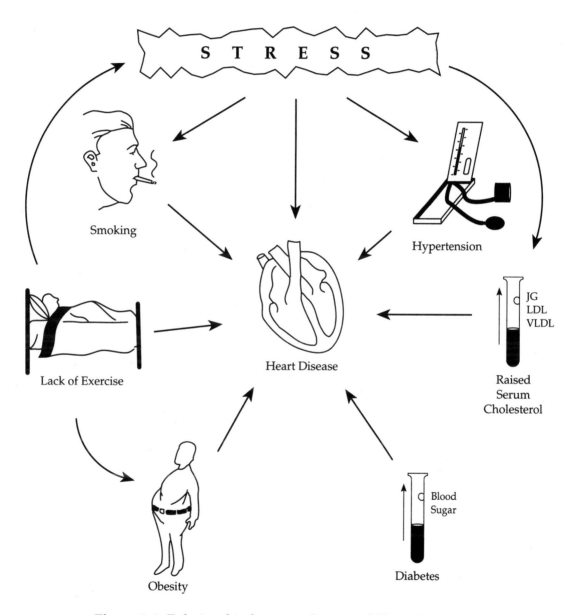

Figure 2-1 Relationship between Stress and Heart Disease

Besides hypertension, coronary heart disease, and stroke; stress is also related as a risk factor to many other physical ailments. Some of these are migraine headaches, peptic ulcers, arthritis, colitis, diarrhea, asthma, cardiac arrhythmias, sexual problems, circulatory problems (cold hands and feet), muscle tension, allergies, backache, temporomandibular joint syndrome and cancer (Greenberg, 1993; Girdano, Everly, Dusek, 1993; Rice, 1992; Smith, 1993). Now with the help of Worksheet 2.2 let us find out whether we experience any manifestations of chronic stress.

Worksheet 2.3 which follows Worksheet 2.2 has been designed to help us reflect on our thoughts in general. Thoughts and ensuing emotions are the most powerful sources of stress and are unfortunately the least emphasized and understood phenomena.

Worksheet 2.2
Do We Suffer from Chronic Stress?

Let us check all the items which apply to us.

_____   1.   I frequently suffer from burning sensation in the upper abdominal region.

_____   2.   I often have difficulty digesting food and have belching.

_____   3.   I often have backache or joint pains.

_____   4.   I frequently suffer from headaches.

_____   5.   I sometimes have chest pain.

_____   6.   I have been diagnosed as having heart disease or hypertension.

_____   7.   I have had a stroke in the past.

_____   8.   I frequently develop cold hands and feet.

_____   9.   I frequently have diarrhea and loose motions, especially when I am anxious.

_____   10.   I suffer from a great deal of anxiety.

FEEDBACK ON WORKSHEET 2.2

If we have checked any of the items, we are likely to be suffering from the effects of chronic stress. Let us not worry! It is still not too late to change our lifestyle.

If we have checked items 1 & 2, then we are likely candidates for <u>peptic ulcer</u> which is precipitated and aggravated by stress. Item 3 pertains to <u>backache</u> and <u>arthritis</u> which have been associated with chronic stress. Item 4 refers to <u>migraine</u> and <u>tension headaches</u> which are a result of stress. Items 5-7 pertain to <u>coronary heart disease</u> and <u>hypertension</u>. Item 8 refers to <u>circulatory problems</u> which are stress related. Item 9 indicates <u>diarrhea</u> and <u>colitis</u> which have been related to stress. Finally, Item 10 pertains to generalized anxiety disorder which is also a result of chronic stress.

If we are young, it is likely that we may not have checked any of the items. This only indicates that we have not yet been invaded by the harmful effects of stress. Therefore, it is all the more a reason for us to practice stress reduction, prevention, and management techniques.

* * * * * * * * * * * * * * *

Worksheet 2.3
Thought Identification

For the next 15 minutes let us leave aside everything we have been doing and try to write down <u>all</u> the thoughts that are coming into our mind in the space provided below. Let us ensure that we write down everything, even if it may appear trivial or unimportant.

_____

_____

_____

_____

_____

_____

_____

_____

_____

_____

_____

_____

_____

_____

_____

_____

_____

_____

_____

FEEDBACK ON WORKSHEET 2.3

See how many thoughts have come to our mind in such a short period of time of just 15 minutes. Let us count these. A multiplication of this figure with four will provide us with the number of thoughts which have come to our mind in an hour. Let us proceed to calculate the total number of thoughts that come to our mind in a year and in an expected lifetime of 75 years.

Number of thoughts in 15 min = (A) = _____

Number of thoughts in 1 hour = (B) = (A x 4) = _____

Number of thoughts in 1 day = (C) = (B x 24) = _____

Number of thoughts in 1 year = (D) = (C x 365) = _____

Number of thoughts in 75 years = (E) = (D x 75) = _____

This is a simplistic calculation. For the sake of simplicity we have included all the time in the day. However, when we are deeply engrossed in certain tasks, or when we are in deep sleep, the number of thoughts decreases. It needs to be noted that, in light sleep while dreaming the frequently of thoughts increases. In essence, this may have a canceling out effect. Therefore, in our calculations we may be close to accuracy owing to a "canceling out" effect.

This can be appreciated that in our lifetime we generate a large number of thoughts and only a few of these are relevant and need to be processed. This approach shall be helpful in order for us to reduce our stress and lead a productive life.

* * * * * * * * * * * * * *

Stress and Expectations

All of us will appreciate that the body has only a limited potential to process a few of the thoughts which come to our mind and most of the unwanted, unprocessed thoughts contribute to our stress levels. Since we cannot do anything about the unwanted, unprocessed thoughts, we need to be selective and judiciously indulge in only those thoughts which we can process. The techniques to reduce these thoughts can only be acquired through proper conditioning of the mind over a period of time. This reduction in the number of unwanted thoughts will most certainly help in reducing our stress levels. How we interpret and label these thoughts is also an important dimension. Let us imagine a situation in which we observe our boss or teacher looking at us in an unusual way. It is easy for us to attribute this look to mean that we are not doing well and this is likely to be stressful and anxiety provoking. Interpretation of the same event as being due to his or her being tired or having personal problems will not cause stress. Brooding over our thoughts or dwelling on our worries only adds to the tension in our body, which in turn creates the subjective feeling of uneasiness and leads to more anxious thoughts. Becoming excessively emotional about these thoughts is another contributing factor to stress. Emotions or feelings are helpful, but if we become unduly emotional, then the emotions do not serve any purpose. Instead these emotions do more harm than good by stimulating the physiological processes and precipitating the stress response. This stress response drains away the vital energy needed by the body to perform important daily functions.

Stress is also the result of our interactions with people, situations, and the environment around us. If we think about people and situations which contribute to our stress, we will find that people who are close to us and situations from which we expect to benefit are the ones which contribute to most of our stress. This stress is tied into the inherent **expectation** which we have from these people and situations. Is this expectation realistic? Most of the time it is not.

We cannot become hermits or renounce the world and escape all stresses of life. However, we can learn to counteract our conventional response to stress by learning how to relax effectively and reducing unwanted thoughts. These techniques help the body in attaining a state of balance or "homeostasis." Relaxation and modification of thoughts restore our lost energy. Before we discuss relaxation techniques, effective communication techniques, methods for managing anger, coping with anxiety, maintaining a balanced diet, ways to exercise regularly, and managing time efficiently by modifying our thought process, we have to enhance our awareness of the type, frequency, intensity, and duration of stress operating in our body. An awareness of any problem is certainly the first step toward aiming at a solution. Therefore, it is important for us to begin examining questions pertaining to what, where, how, and when before we begin searching for a solution. The worksheets which follow are aimed at achieving an enhancement of our awareness about stress. Let us now complete the following worksheets.

Worksheet 2.4
Stress Awareness Log

Principles

A daily record of stressors can serve as a valuable tool in learning to cope with stress. Keeping a stress record through log sheets is an excellent tool for this purpose. The stress awareness log serves three important purposes:

1. Helps to familiarize how we respond to stress.
2. Helps to rule out other than stress related causes to any symptoms we might have.
3. Helps in establishing some baseline data and developing goals for ourselves in reducing stress.

Initially, maintaining this stress awareness log may appear complicated and time-consuming; however, it is not so. Once we have used this "means of record keeping" with log sheets for a few days and we become familiar with their use, it will take us only a few minutes of our time every day.

The information which we record on the stress log sheets is for our use only. We need not share it with anyone. It is important that we be <u>candid and honest</u> with ourselves in filling out these log sheets. If our daily experiences remain unclear, then the means for finding appropriate solutions will also be hazy. It is important that we maintain the log sheets for <u>at least 4-5 consecutive days</u>. Let us try to include a weekend in our recordings, as we normally tend to behave differently over weekends and sometimes this difference may result in contributing to our stress.

The most important part of the stress awareness log is for us to maintain it <u>conscientiously</u>. It is a very effective tool to help us identify ways in which we respond to stress. However, unless we maintain it accurately and work at it, it will be of no value and may even contribute to increasing our stress levels. The more information we put into this stress awareness log, the more we will benefit from it in the long run.

Recording Instructions

In the headings outlined below, we will have to make a record on the log sheets as described.

<u>Time of the day</u>. Includes a serial record of time for each event chronologically. We need to use one log sheet per day, so five such sheets have been provided. However, if we want to maintain the recording over a longer period of time, then we can make photocopies of these sheets.

Worksheet 2. 4 Stress Awareness Log (Cont'd)

Signals. These are indicators, manifestations, signs, symptoms, responses, reactions (e.g. physical - headache, muscle tension, perspiration, palpitation or rapid heart rate; mental - loss of attention span, poor concentration, effect on memory, impaired judgement; behavioral - inability to interact with others, uncontrolled anger, reduced job performance).

Stressors. These are events which can be looked upon as "inputs" originating from our thoughts, situations, and the environment. If the event causes stress or interferes with one's ability to accomplish daily tasks, then it is stressor. It is also important to consider differing intensity levels of various stressors.

How am I dealing with the stressors? In this section we record techniques and mechanisms, if any, that we have been using in handling the stressors. It would also be worthwhile to record the time of the day the technique was used or mechanism operated. Also record whether or not it made any difference.

How effective have I been? / What else can I do? This section would include whether or not we were able to work with the stressor in a satisfactory way and whether or not the means of resolution worked. Any other comments, if necessary, may be added in this section.

Now we can begin recording on the sheets for at least four to five consecutive days. We may also like to prepare a brief summary statement of the information entered on our log sheets, if we need to share it with someone else, or if we want concise information from these recordings for greater insight.

Worksheet 2. 4 Stress Awareness Log (Cont'd)

Day & Date: _____

TIME OF THE DAY	SIGNALS	STRESSOR	HOW AM I DEALING WITH THE STRESSORS?	HOW EFFECTIVE HAVE I BEEN? WHAT ELSE CAN I DO?

Worksheet 2. 4 Stress Awareness Log (Cont'd)

Day & Date: _____

TIME OF THE DAY	SIGNALS	STRESSOR	HOW AM I DEALING WITH THE STRESSORS?	HOW EFFECTIVE HAVE I BEEN? WHAT ELSE CAN I DO?

Worksheet 2. 4 Stress Awareness Log (Cont'd)

Day & Date: _____

TIME OF THE DAY	SIGNALS	STRESSOR	HOW AM I DEALING WITH THE STRESSORS?	HOW EFFECTIVE HAVE I BEEN? WHAT ELSE CAN I DO?

Worksheet 2. 4 Stress Awareness Log (Cont'd)

Day & Date: _____

TIME OF THE DAY	SIGNALS	STRESSOR	HOW AM I DEALING WITH THE STRESSORS?	HOW EFFECTIVE HAVE I BEEN? WHAT ELSE CAN I DO?

Worksheet 2. 4 Stress Awareness Log (Cont'd)

Day & Date: _____

TIME OF THE DAY	SIGNALS	STRESSOR	HOW AM I DEALING WITH THE STRESSORS?	HOW EFFECTIVE HAVE I BEEN? WHAT ELSE CAN I DO?

FEEDBACK ON WORKSHEET 2.4

Maintaining a stress awareness log is an excellent tool which provides us with accurate feedback on our present stress levels. If it is maintained carefully and honestly, it generates useful insights into our own behavior which forms an important basis for initiating change in our lifestyle. It also provides us with an opportunity to look at our unhealthy lifestyles which are jeopardizing our own health. It is an important first step to initiate any subsequent changes.

In order to interpret the information from the Stress Awareness Log we need to be objective. We need to critically appraise our behavior and identify as to what changes can be easily and effectively incorporated into our daily lifestyle. In subsequent chapters of this Workbook these changes have been elaborated on step by step.

* * * * * * * * * * * * * *

Worksheet 2.5
Stress & Tension Test

Recalling our memory for the past one month, let us try to answer the following questions as honestly as possible. Circle responses.

No.	Item	Always	Often	Sometimes	Rarely
1.	I feel tense, anxious, and uptight.	3	2	1	0
2.	I cannot stop worrying at night, and during my leisure time.	3	2	1	0
3.	I have headaches, backache, and pain in the shoulder or neck.	3	2	1	0
4.	My sleep is disrupted and I usually keep getting up while sleeping.	3	2	1	0
5.	People around me tend to cause me stress and make me irritable.	3	2	1	0
6.	I tend to eat, drink, and/or smoke in response to my stress and anxiety.	3	2	1	0
7.	I do not feel refreshed in the mornings and am normally tired, lethargic and exhausted during the day.	3	2	1	0
8.	I find it difficult to concentrate on my tasks and activities which I am supposed to perform.	3	2	1	0

Worksheet 2.5 Stress & Tension Test (Cont'd)

No.	Item	Always	Often	Sometimes	Rarely
9.	I have to use tranquilizers, sedatives or other drugs to relax me.	3	2	1	0
10.	I do not find time to relax.	3	2	1	0
11.	I have too many deadlines to meet and I fall behind in accomplishing them.	3	2	1	0

Note. From John. W. Farquhar, M.D., The American way of life need not be hazardous to your health, Revised Edition, ©1987 by the Stanford Alumni Association. Adapted by permission of Addison-Wesley Publishing Company, Inc.

FEEDBACK ON WORKSHEET 2.5

This instrument helps us to reflect retrospectively, how our present life has been during the past one month. If we have a score over 22, then we certainly have been having high stress levels and we need to work at getting relaxed by practicing stress management techniques. We may also require help from others. If our scores are below 22, then we may not be as much stressed at present, but in order to continue being relaxed and stress free, we need to practice stress management, reduction, and prevention techniques.

* * * * * * * * * * * * * *

Worksheet 2.6
Personal Stress Test

This test is designed to help us assess the impact of stress at this point in our life. Our response to each statement can provide information to help us deal with stress. This test does not assess physical, mental, or emotional illness. It is designed for normal, healthy individuals who want to control stress in a positive manner and enjoy life more.

Let us fill out the test when we are certain not to be interrupted. Let us respond to each statement using the scale to the right of each page. There are no right or wrong answers. Some statements may seem hard to respond to because they are subjective. If none of the available responses appears to fit perfectly, let us pick the one closest to the way we feel. We need not consult the test feedback sheet until we have finished the test. While it is not mandatory to respond to any item we find objectionable, results from completed tests are more accurate. Thus, we need to complete the entire test.

Let us circle one letter to the right of each statement that best describes us and how often we feel that way. Let us answer each statement honestly. If we do not, we are cheating only ourselves.

PROFILE CODE: N = Almost n ever, R = Rarely, S = Sometimes, O = Often, A = Almost always

PROFILE QUESTIONS:

1.	There are situations in which I cannot be myself.	N	R	S	O	A
2.	I have the stamina and endurance I need.	N	R	S	O	A
3.	I worry about how things will turn out.	N	R	S	O	A
4.	I am happy and content.	N	R	S	O	A
5.	I feel motivated to do things.	N	R	S	O	A
6.	I feel sad and down in the dumps.	N	R	S	O	A
7.	I feel in control of my appetite.	N	R	S	O	A
8.	I am sluggish and lack energy.	N	R	S	O	A
9.	I feel loved by someone important to me.	N	R	S	O	A
10.	I feel well-organized and clear-headed.	N	R	S	O	A
11.	My life lacks stimulation.	N	R	S	O	A
12.	Day-to-day living is monotonous for me.	N	R	S	O	A
13.	I accomplish things that are important to me.	N	R	S	O	A
14.	I feel physically strong and capable.	N	R	S	O	A
15.	I fit in well with the people around me.	N	R	S	O	A
16.	I feel resentment about things that have happened to me in the past.	N	R	S	O	A
17.	I enjoy being with the people around me.	N	R	S	O	A

Worksheet 2.6 Personal Stress Test (Cont'd)

18.	There is a difference between how I think I should be and how I am.	N R S O A
19.	My stomach bothers me.	N R S O A
20.	I am lonely.	N R S O A
21.	I think I am living fully.	N R S O A
22.	I have the standard of living I deserve.	N R S O A
23.	I feel excluded by people.	N R S O A
24.	I have difficulty concentrating.	N R S O A
25.	I feel relaxed.	N R S O A
26.	I feel guilty about eating.	N R S O A
27.	I have a clear conscience.	N R S O A
28.	I have aches and pains.	N R S O A
29.	I would like to start all over.	N R S O A
30.	I have pleasant feelings.	N R S O A
31.	It is hard for me to get close to people.	N R S O A
32.	I worry about my weight.	N R S O A
33.	I feel I belong.	N R S O A
34.	I feel like I am part of a family.	N R S O A
35.	My life is dull and uninteresting.	N R S O A
36.	Things that happen to me are unfair.	N R S O A
37.	I can remember important things.	N R S O A
38.	I feel nervous or upset.	N R S O A
39.	I feel good about my eating habits.	N R S O A
40.	I get what I want.	N R S O A

FEEDBACK ON WORKSHEET 2.6

1. Let us place our Personal Stress Test alongside the following answer key.

2. This answer key is divided into ten categories.

   NOTE: THE ORDER OF THE ITEMS ON THIS
   ANSWER KEY IS NOT THE SAME
   AS THE ORDER ON THE TEST.

3. To find the score for each item, let us carefully circle the number below the letter we chose on our stress test.

4. Let us enter the score for each question in the proper bracket under the Total Points column.

5. Let us then total the score for each category on the following page.

Feedback on Worksheet 2.6 (Cont'd)

Stress Factor	Ques. No.	Scoring Key N R S O A	Total Points
1. Physical Condition	2. 8. 14. 28.	5 4 3 2 1 1 2 3 4 5 5 4 3 2 1 1 2 3 4 5	_____ _____ _____ _____ _____
		SubTotal	_____
2. Mental Performance	3. 10. 24. 37.	1 2 3 4 5 5 4 3 2 1 1 2 3 4 5 5 4 3 2 1	_____ _____ _____ _____
		SubTotal	_____
3. Emotional Relaxation	19. 25. 30. 38.	1 2 3 4 5 5 4 3 2 1 5 4 3 2 1 1 2 3 4 5	_____ _____ _____ _____
		SubTotal	_____
4. Weight Control & Image	7. 26. 32. 39.	5 4 3 2 1 1 2 3 4 5 1 2 3 4 5 5 4 3 2 1	_____ _____ _____ _____
		SubTotal	_____
5. Sense of Belonging	15. 20. 33. 34.	5 4 3 2 1 1 2 3 4 5 5 4 3 2 1 5 4 3 2 1	_____ _____ _____ _____
		SubTotal	_____
6. Sense of Relationship	9. 17. 23. 31.	5 4 3 2 1 5 4 3 2 1 1 2 3 4 5 1 2 3 4 5	_____ _____ _____ _____
		SubTotal	_____

Feedback on Worksheet 2.6 (Cont'd)

	Stress Factor	Ques. No.	Scoring Key N R S O A					Total Points
7.	Sense of Satisfaction	4.	5	4	3	2	1	_____
		21.	5	4	3	2	1	_____
		29.	1	2	3	4	5	_____
		35.	1	2	3	4	5	_____
					SubTotal			_____
8.	Sense of Integrity	1.	1	2	3	4	5	_____
		13.	5	4	3	2	1	_____
		18.	1	2	3	4	5	_____
		27.	5	4	3	2	1	_____
					SubTotal			_____
9.	Sense of Justice	16.	1	2	3	4	5	_____
		22.	5	4	3	2	1	_____
		36.	1	2	3	4	5	_____
		40.	5	4	3	2	1	_____
					SubTotal			_____
10.	Sense of Stimulation	5.	5	4	3	2	1	_____
		6.	1	2	3	4	5	_____
		11.	1	2	3	4	5	_____
		12.	1	2	3	4	5	_____
					SubTotal			_____

Now transfer these scores to the following sheet to obtain your Personal Stress Profile.

Feedback on Worksheet 2.6 (Cont'd)

Let us transfer the subtotal scores calculated above for each category under the subtotal scores column below. Let us then place an "X" on the adjoining scale. This scale visually reveals our areas of low, moderate, and high stress in these categories.

Stress Profile Factor	SubTotal Scores	S C A L E					
		Low		Moderate		High	
		0	4	8	12	16	20
1. Physical Condition	_____						
2. Mental Performance	_____						
3. Emotional Relaxation	_____						
4. Weight Control & Image	_____						
5. Sense of Belonging	_____						
6. Sense of Relationship	_____						
7. Sense of Satisfaction	_____						
8. Sense of Integrity	_____						
9. Sense of Justice	_____						
10. Sense of Stimulation	_____						

Feedback on Worksheet 2.6 (Cont'd)

Interpretation of Scores:

Factor	High 12-20 (Poor Coping)	COMMON INDICATORS Moderate 9-11 (Dissatisfaction)	Low 4-8 (Good Coping)
1. Physical Condition	• Aches, pains • Fatigue • Listlessness • Illness prone	• Energy level fluctuations • Little stamina	• Stamina • Strength • Active
2. Mental Perform	• Forgets details • Worries a lot • Ruminates	• Confusion • Mind vacillates • Details escape	• Clarity • Solves problems • Concentrate
3. Emotional Relaxation	• Tense • Nervous • Anxious • Sleeplessness • Stomach churnings	• Irritable • Inner turmoil • Some tension	• Calm • Confident • Relaxed
4. Weight Control & Image	• Eats more • Disappointed with image	• Eats too much or too little • Not satisfied with image	• Eats when hungry • Balanced diet
5. Sense of Belonging	• Alienated • Loneliness • Separation	• Close to only few • Distant with others	• Common bonds with many • Comfortable with others
6. Sense of Relation	• Tense relations • Withdrawal	• Shares little about self • Few inquiries about others • Unpredictable	• Strong friendships • Long term relations
7. Sense of satisfaction	• Wanting to start life over	• Unsure • Questions • Disinterested • Discontent	• Happy • Contented • Enthusiasm • Fulfillment

Feedback on Worksheet 2.6 (Cont'd)

COMMON INDICATORS

Factor	High 12-20 (Poor Coping)	Moderate 9-11 (Dissatisfaction)	Low 4-8 (Good Coping)
8. Sense of Integrity	• Reserved • Unsure • Expedient	• Inconsistent • Regrets behavior • Attitude of martyrdom	• Acts on priorities • Able to say no • Pride in accomplishment
9. Sense of Justice	• Resentment • Anger • Incapable	• Roll with punches • Questions	• Control • Fairness • Balance
10. Sense of Stimulate	• Monotony • Boredom • Laziness	• Moderate interest in life • Future has appeal	• Enthusiasm • Motivation • Takes initiative

* * * * * * * * * * * * * * *

Thoughts for Reflection 2.1

Commitment

- Is it not true that commitment is vital to the success of any task!

- Let us imagine all our past successes. Were we not committed to the tasks?

- Does commitment not reduce stress?

- If we are committed, would that not reduce the chances of self-doubt, failure and inefficiency? Would that not in turn reduce stress?

- What if we are not committed? Would that not add to the confusion of roles which we perform? Would that not contribute to purposelessness and lack of direction?

* * * * * * * * * * * * * *

Thoughts for Reflection 2.2

True Happiness or *"Ananda"*

True happiness or *"Ananda"* only arises by focusing on the present. If we can be happy now, then we have learned to be happy anytime. However, if we choose to believe that we will be happy . . .

• if . . .   • when . . .   • with . . .   • only if . . .   • in . . .

Then, we are only making our happiness contingent on external things. We may become happy temporarily, but true happiness will elude us. True happiness or *"ananda"* is an internal feeling which cannot be dependent on any external object. This understanding has to be appreciated by us and also implemented in our daily life. We have to constantly keep reminding ourselves that true happiness or *"ananda"* is an internal phenomenon not dependent on the outside world. We have to learn to be happy, . . . "just happy" and not happy . . . "due to."

* * * * * * * * * * * * * *

Stress Management Principle # 2

We need to become aware before considering change

Summary Points

- For any change to occur besides knowledge, an enhanced awareness is essential.

- Stress affects all of us. We all experience acute and chronic manifestations of stress.

- The acute manifestations of stress present themselves either predominantly on the body, or primarily on the mind. For some, there may be a mixed reaction on both the body and mind.

- Diseases like backache, arthritis, colitis, hypertension, coronary heart disease, stroke, headache, migraine, temporomandibular joint syndrome, circulatory problems, anxiety, asthma, and peptic ulcer have been found to be associated with stress.

- Maintaining a daily observation of the stress in our lives is the first and foremost step in dealing with stress.

- Commitment to alleviating stress is a vital prerequisite for initiating stress management programs.

References and Further Readings

Becker, M. H. (1974). The health belief model and personal health behavior. <u>Health Education Monographs</u>, <u>2</u>, 324-473.

Donatelle, R. J., & Davis, L. G. (1993). <u>Access to health</u>. (Brief 2nd ed.). Englewood Cliffs, NJ: Prentice Hall.

Farquahar, J. W. (1979). <u>The American way of life need not be hazardous to your health</u>. New York, NY: W. W. Norton Co., Inc.

Girdano, D. A., Everly, G. S. Jr., & Dusek, D. E. (1993). <u>Controlling stress and tension: A holistic approach</u>. Englewood Cliffs, NJ: Prentice Hall.

Green, L. W., & Kreuter, M. W. (1991). <u>Health promotion planning: An educational and environmental approach</u>. (2nd ed.). Mountain View, CA: Mayfield Publishing Company.

Greenberg, J. S. (1993). <u>Comprehensive stress management</u>. (4th ed.). Dubuque, IA: William C. Brown Publishers.

Greenberg, J.S., & Dintiman, G.B. (1992). <u>Exploring health. Expanding the boundaries of wellness</u>. Englewood Cliffs, NJ: Prentice Hall.

Rice, P. L. (1992). <u>Stress and health</u>. (2nd ed.). Pacific Grove, CA: Brooks/Cole Publishing Company.

Smith, J. C. (1993). <u>Understanding stress and coping</u>. New York, NY: Macmillan Publishing Company.

CHAPTER 3

RELAXATION

Sleep

Come, Sleep! O Sleep, the certain knot of peace,
The baiting-place of wit, the balm of woe,
The poor man's wealth, the prisoner's release,
Th' indifferent judge between the high and low.

Sir Philip Sidney
(Astrophel and Stella, Sonnet 39)

What Is Relaxation?

The word relax is derived from the Latin word *relaxare* meaning to loosen. Indeed relaxation implies loosening up or letting go. By this process of relaxing or loosening, all living beings consolidate and restore energy which has been lost in daily activities. Therefore, relaxation is vital for the normal functioning of any living organism. Relaxation techniques form the core of all stress management programs. When our bodies are functioning normally, we derive relaxation through sleep.

Sleep

We all sleep. Without sleep we cannot live, although there may be some exceptions. Sleep accomplishes two vital functions — conservation of energy and restoration of energy (Shapiro & Flanigan, 1993). Expenditure of energy is mainly measured by the metabolic rate (in simple terms, the rate of conversion of ingested food into energy useful for the body), which is raised during the day and reduced during the night (particularly during sleep) by between 5.0% and 25.0% (Shapiro & Flanigan, 1993). Physiologically, sleep is composed of two phases:

1. Non REM (Rapid Eye Movement) Sleep.

This is the sleep phase characterized by four stages:
• Stage 1 is a light, drowsy phase of Non REM sleep (the transition from wakefulness to sleep). Electroencephalogram is a scientific method which helps to gauge the electrical impulses within the brain with the help of the electrodes placed over the scalp. Normally if this electroencephalogram (EEG) recording is done during the awake state, when our mind and senses are working, then this recording will manifest beta waves (fast waves at a rhythm of 14 to 40 cycles per second). As drowsiness sets in, the frequency of beta waves starts to recede.
• Stage 2 is the first real stage of sleep which is characterized by "spindles" and "K complexes" on an EEG. During this stage of Non REM phase sleep, the EEG will record alpha waves (slower waves at 8-13 cycles per second). In this stage, the mind comes to a peaceful state.

• <u>Stages 3 & 4</u> are known as "slow wave sleep." In these stages of Non REM phase of sleep the mind gets subtler and EEG records theta waves (4-7 cycles per second). In extremely deep sleep or coma, the EEG records delta waves (near 1 cycle per second).

2. <u>REM (Rapid Eye Movement) Sleep</u>.

This is the phase of sleep during which most dreaming happens. It occurs approximately 90 minutes after the person falls asleep. During this stage the mind functions at alpha and beta waves. From a relaxation perspective, during this phase a person does not actually get relaxed. However, this is still an important phase of sleep.

There is a cycle of Non REM and REM sleep throughout the night. As the night progresses, the episodes of Non REM sleep become shorter, and those of the REM phase of sleep longer. Most slow wave sleep occurs during the first third of the night, and most REM sleep during the last third of sleep (Kalat, 1988).

However, when we are stressed, our normal biorhythm is altered and our sleep pattern is disturbed. Therefore, our bodies are not able to conserve and restore the lost energy. This in turn adds to the stress and a vicious cycle is set up. If this disturbed sleep pattern is not changed, or relaxation methods are not used, complete balance and harmony is disrupted.

It may even be the other way around. If, for reasons of overwork or not being able to find enough time, we sleep less, our biorhythm gets altered. Therefore, the body needs other forms of relaxation in order to conserve and restore lost energy.

Relaxation Techniques

Relaxation techniques provide us with excellent methods which can be practiced with awareness at our discretion anytime. This is especially important when we are just beginning to experience stress. In this case, most of the negative consequences of stress can be counteracted even before they have occurred.

Various techniques have been suggested in order to achieve relaxation. In this workbook the methods of Yogic Breathing, Progressive Muscle Relaxation, Autogenic Training, and Visual Imagery will be described in detail. Other techniques of relaxation like Yoga, Meditation, and Biofeedback are also introduced in this workbook. However, these methods require personal instruction and supervision by a qualified and experienced person. Thus the actual techniques for these have not been completely elaborated, and the reader is provided with appropriate resources for obtaining further assistance.

Yoga and Meditation

Fundamentally, relaxation techniques owe their origin to Eastern cultures, particularly India. They are a part of the overall system of "Yoga" which originated from the *Vedas*. The word "Yoga" is derived from the Sanskrit root meaning "union" implying the joining or yoking of human consciousness to the Divine Being. According to

Webster's New World Dictionary (1991), Yoga is a mystic and ascetic Hindu discipline by which one seeks to achieve liberation of the self and union with the supreme spirit or universal soul through intense concentration, deep meditation, and practices involving prescribed postures, controlled breathing, and so on. It is a complete system of physical, mental, social, and spiritual development of the human being. A contemporary description of Yoga is "a systematic practice and implementation of mind and body in the living process of human beings to keep harmony within self, within society, and with nature" (Maharishi, 1986, 1987, 1989).

For generations this philosophy was passed on from the master teacher to the student. The first written records about this methodology appeared around 200 BC in *Yogasutra* of Patanjali. It was known as *"Asthangayoga"* or the eightfold path of physical, psychological, and moral discipline, that if properly adhered to, under the guidance of a qualified teacher, results in enhancement of purity and improved stress-coping skills (Singh, 1983). This eightfold path of *Asthangayoga* consists of the following:

(1) *Yama:* Restraints or rules for living in society. For example, truthfulness, non injury, non stealing, etc

(2) *Niyama:* Observances or rules for self. For example, contentment, cleanliness, etc.

(3) *Asaana:* Physical exercises

(4) *Pranayama:* Regulated breathing practice

(5) *Pratihara:* Detaching the mind from senses

(6) *Dharana:* Concentration on an object, internal or external

(7) *Dhyana:* Meditation

(8) *Samadhi:* Deep meditation on cosmic

The above process involves arousal of the *Kundalini Shakti,* or serpent power, believed to be located at the base of the human spine. As the practitioner practices the various techniques, this power rises through a series of centers or *Chakras* corresponding to various endocrine glands. When this power reaches the highest center, *Sahasrara,* which is associated with the hypothalamus gland regulating the hormonal secretion of the endocrine glands, a control over the hypothalamus results. This way secretion of hormones from various endocrine glands can be regulated. This mechanism could possibly explain the important role that this method plays in coping with stress.

In the past Yoga was a very strict and tedious process and was confined to only a select few. However, later many teachers modified the techniques and various paths emerged like, *"Bhakti Yoga,"* the path of devotion; *"Gyana Yoga,"* the path of knowledge; *"Raja Yoga,"* the path of wisdom to self realization and enlightenment; and *"Karma Yoga,"* the path of action. Various intermediary techniques like *Hatha Yoga, Mudra Yoga, Chakra Yoga,* etc. have also gained popularity.

The system of Yoga is in the process of developing as a science. Various techniques of Yoga have developed and become popular all over the world, particularly in the West, which are, in comparison to the old methods, more simple. Examples of prevalent systems in the West include Transcendental Meditation (TM), *Kriya Yoga,* and Simplified Kundalini Yoga (SKY).

Transcendental Meditation (TM) was developed by Maharishi Mahesh Yogi, disciple of Brahmananda Saraswati, in the year 1957. In 1971 he founded the Maharishi International University in Fairfield, Iowa. In 1975 he established the International Capital of the Age of Enlightenment at Seelisberg in Switzerland, which has now been renamed Maharishi European Research University. It is a simple, natural technique that can be learned by any person belonging to any age, education, occupation, or cultural background. TM has to be practiced everyday for 15 to 20 minutes and requires personal instruction by a qualified master who can gauge normal progress and take care of any adverse experiences if they arise. The centers teaching this technique are established all over the world and the process consists of the following seven steps (Kumar, 1993):

1. Introductory lecture - a vision of the possibilities through TM (60 minutes).

2. Preparatory lecture - the origin and mechanics of TM (60 minutes).

3. Personal interview with the teacher (15 minutes).

4. Personal instruction - learning the technique (60 minutes).

5. Verification and validation of experiences - verifying the correctness of the practice (90 minutes).

6. Understanding the mechanics of stabilizing the benefits of TM (90 minutes).

7. Understanding the mechanics of development of higher states of consciousness through TM (90 minutes).

Further information about Transcendental Meditation can be obtained from: Transcendental Meditation National Center, 13039 Ventura Blvd., Los Angeles, CA 90024, (213) 463-8970.

Kriya Yoga became popular in the West due to the efforts of Paramhansa Yogananda, who founded the Yogoda Satsanga Society in India, and Self-Realization Fellowship in the United States of America. The word *"Kriya"* is derived from the Sanskrit root *kri* meaning "to do," "to act," and "to react." This method of *Kriya Yoga* involves a psychophysiological method by which human blood is decarbonated and recharged with oxygen. This extra oxygen is converted into life current to rejuvenate the central nervous system, lessen and prevent the decay of tissues, and enhance evolution of the mind (Yogananda, 1946). Further information on this technique and system can be obtained from Self-Realization Fellowship, 3880 San Rafael Avenue, Los Angeles, CA 90065.

A better and more refined system is Yogiraj Vethathiri Maharishi's Simplified Kundalini Yoga (SKY). Yogiraj Vethathiri Maharishi formed the World Community Service Center in 1958. This system was developed as a result of many years of extensive practice and research (Maharishi, 1986, 1987, 1989). It involves the arousal, awakening, and development of *Kundalini Shakti,* which lies dormant in most individuals at *Mooladhara,* at the base of the spine. The energy levels are raised to *Agna Chakra* and then to *Sahasrara.* The important aspect of this system is *Shanti Yoga* which helps keep control of the powerful awakened *Kundalini Shakti.* Other important aspects of this system include simplified physical exercises, introspection, or analysis of thoughts (as described in Chapter 6), and *Kaya Kalpa* which is a system of exercises designed to improve upon health and longevity.   Interested readers can contact the organization headquarters at the following addresses: World Community Service Center, 20 Second Seaward Street, Valmiki Nagar, Thiruvanmiyur, Madras 600 041, India, or in the United States at World Community Service Center of California, 926 La Rambla, Burbank, CA 91501, (818) 848-1509; Toma and Adele Fitzgerald, 12205 Gorham, No. 4, Brentwood, CA 90049, (310) 207-4871; Ram Patil, 9343 Larch, Munster, IN 46321, (219) 924-6301; Dr. V.K. Gupta, 100 Old Sunshine Trail, Boulder, CO (303) 440-5895.

Other systems of meditation include (Naranjo & Ornstein, 1971):

- Soto Zen, which involves focusing on external objects,

- Rinzai Zen, in which the mind has to focus on koans (unanswerable, illogical riddles),

- Zazen, in which the mind has to focus on subjective states of consciousness, and

- Tibetian Meditation, in which the mind has to focus on geometrical figures .

Yogic Breathing or *"Pranayama"*

All of us breathe. Breathing is a vital function for life. However, we seldom pay attention to how we breathe. This is an important aspect and needs to be understood. The process of breathing has received special emphasis in the system of Yoga. As mentioned earlier, this process is known as *Pranayama*. The purpose of this technique is not only to increase the vital capacity of the lungs, but also to enhance the oxygenation capacity of the blood by the lungs. The oxygen from the air which we breathe in is carried by the hemoglobin in the blood to the various parts of the body for providing energy. If greater oxygen can be carried by the blood, then greater restoration of energy which has been lost in daily activities can be achieved. Therefore, the process of Yogic breathing or *pranayama* is essential for achieving relaxation and managing stress.   In simple terms, Yogic breathing consists of three stages (Vasu, 1915):

- *Puraka* (inhalation)

- *Kumbhaka* (pausing or holding the breath)

- *Rechaka* (exhalation)

The ratio of these three stages is 1: 4: 2 — that is, if one inhales the air for four seconds, then the person has to hold the air for sixteen seconds, and then exhale the air over a period of eight seconds. The purpose of Yogic breathing or *Pranayama* is to achieve this kind of rhythmic breathing. We sometimes achieve this kind of breathing pattern when we are engrossed in some task with deep concentration, or some of us may be naturally gifted with this kind of pattern. This type of breathing pattern helps the body to relax and conserve energy. It has been found to be useful in curing chronic muscle fatigue, migraine and tension headaches, and other stress related disorders. Worksheet 3.1 which follows is based upon the traditional basic principles of Yogic breathing but has been slightly modified to suit the feasibility in modern times and its universal applicability. Pregnant women are however advised not to follow this technique during the course of their pregnancy and post partum period, because it may cause unwanted pressure and/or hormonal changes which may affect the growing fetus.

Thoughts for Reflection 3.1 help us to reflect upon some of the barriers which may be hindering us from getting enough relaxation.

Thoughts for Reflection 3.1

Barriers to Relaxation

Reflect upon the following barriers which might be hindering our path to relaxing effectively.

- Working for Long Hours. Some of us, in our quest to earn greater material wealth or for other reasons, may be working more than what is normally required. This may be providing us with less time to relax.

- Brooding. Repetitive thinking of the same thoughts over and over again is brooding. It is often counterproductive. It is a barrier in the way for us to relax.

- Unchecked Imagination. If we do not put a restriction to our imagination, then we may generate thousands of ideas in a short time which is an important barrier to relaxation.

- Heavy Meals.   Eating more than what is required for maintaining the functioning of our body often results in indigestion. It also liberates greater energy. These factors hinder effective relaxation.

- Inefficient Time Management. Planning our time well is very important. If we do not provide ourselves with adequate time for relaxation we shall not be able to relax properly.

- Not Enough Faith in the Power of Relaxation. It is essential for any method to be really effective if it commands respect and faith from those utilizing it. Some of us do not have enough faith in the power of relaxation which colors our perspective and prevents us from getting complete relaxation.

Worksheet 3.1
Yogic Breathing or *"Pranayama"*

This technique can be practiced at any time, but the person should not have taken food over the past two hours. The best time to perform this is early morning on an empty stomach and/or evening before supper. Pregnant women should <u>not</u> do this during the course of their pregnancy or immediate post partal period.

A. <u>Basic Breathing</u>

<u>Step 1</u>.   Let us sit down in a relaxed posture. The ideal posture is squatting with the legs crossed. Let us place a watch in front of us.

<u>Step 2</u>.   Let us inhale deeply and slowly. As we inhale, let us fill in our lungs completely, starting from the lower section to the middle, and proceeding to the upper section. Let us mentally record the time of completing the inhalation. Usually for beginners this time could range from anywhere between four to sixteen seconds. With practice this time can be increased. Though, traditionally, there is no limit to the time, we would recommend that one does not exceed twenty seconds for the process of inhalation without supervision from an experienced practitioner.

<u>Step 3</u>.   Let us hold the breath for a duration of four times the amount of time which we had taken for completing the inhalation.

<u>Step 4</u>.   Let us exhale the air slowly in a time which is twice the time we had taken to complete inhaling or which is half the time which we had taken in holding the breath.

<u>Step 5</u>.   Let us repeat Steps 3-5 for five times over the first week. Then gradually increase the number of times over a period of the next few months. We would recommend that practice in one sitting does not exceed more than fifty times and not more than two times a day at that level without supervision from an experienced practitioner.

Worksheet 3.1   Yogic Breathing or _"Pranayama"_   (Cont'd)

B. <u>Bending Breathing</u>

<u>Step 1</u>. Let us kneel down on our knees or stand up straight.

<u>Step 2</u>. Let us inhale slowly and completely. Let us first fill in the lower section of the lungs, then the middle and finally the upper section.

<u>Step 3</u>. While bending down from our original position let us gradually exhale the air completely. We may take approximately the same amount of time which we took for inhaling.

<u>Step 4</u>. While rising up from your original position let us gradually inhale and fill our lungs completely.

<u>Step 5</u>. Repeat Steps 3-4 five times for the first week. We may then gradually increase our frequency over the next couple of months. Again we would recommend a maximum of twenty times twice a day.

C. <u>Alternative Breathing</u>

<u>Step 1</u>. Let us sit in a comfortable position.

<u>Step 2</u>. Let us close our right nostril with the thumb of our right hand.

<u>Step 3</u>. Let us inhale air slowly and completely through our left nostril.

<u>Step 4</u>. Let us exhale air slowly and completely through our left nostril.

<u>Step 5</u>. Let us repeat Steps 2-4 five times.

<u>Step 6</u>. Let us close our left nostril with the index and middle fingers of our right hand.

<u>Step 7</u>. Let us inhale air slowly and completely through our right nostril.

Worksheet 3.1 Yogic Breathing or *"Pranayama"*   (Cont'd)

Step 8.   Let us exhale air slowly and completely through our right nostril.

Step 9.   Let us repeat Steps 6-8 five times.

Step 10.   In this step we have to practice alternative breathing. Close our right nostril with our right thumb and   inhale air slowly and completely through our left nostril. As soon as we complete inhalation, close our left nostril with the index and middle fingers of our right hand. Let us exhale air through the right nostril.

Step 11.   Let us repeat Step 10 five times.

Step 12.   Let us close our left nostril with the index and middle fingers of our right hand. Let us inhale air slowly and completely through our right nostril. As soon as we complete inhalation, let us close our right nostril with the thumb of our right hand. Let us exhale air through our left nostril.

Step 13.   Let us repeat Step 12 five times.

FEEDBACK ON WORKSHEET 3.1

This is a practice based technique and has to be practiced regularly. We may do it once a day or two times. We need not exceed the maximal frequency. This is a useful technique, which if practiced regularly can modify the conventional "fight or flight" response to stress and reduce undue anxiety. Once we have mastered the yogic breathing technique it can also be easily practiced to relieve stress. All we need to do is sit down and perform yogic breathing whenever we are stressed. A couple of breaths taken in will rechannelize the response and reduce the negative stimulation associated with stress.

* * * * * * * * * * * * * * *

Biofeedback

Biofeedback has been defined as the use of instrumentation to mirror psychological processes of which the individual is not normally aware and which may be brought under voluntary control (Brown, 1974; Fuller, 1977; Karlins & Andrews, 1972). The primary objective of biofeedback is monitoring and modification of the psychophysiological response which is obtained by enhancing awareness of internal states connected with deep levels of relaxation. Usually, information about internal vital functions such as blood pressure, heart rhythm, muscle tension, and so on, is electronically recorded. This information is then explained to the participant who is then encouraged to gradually work at modifying the responses by exerting greater relaxation. Gradually the participant is enabled to gain greater modifying power on these internal functions which contribute to the reduction of stress. It is normally administered with the help of a therapist.   Sessions of one hour each last anywhere from 10 to 40 in number. The process involves three phases:

- Measurement of psychophysiological parameters.

- Conversion of these into simple, understandable forms.

- Feedback of this information to the participant.

Some of the instruments utilized in biofeedback laboratories are the Electromyograph (EMG), which measures muscle tension and relaxation; Thermal Units, which measure skin surface temperature; Electroencephalograph (EEG), which measures brain wave activity monitored from sensors placed on the scalp; and Galvanic Skin Response (GSR) Units, which measure sympathetic nervous system changes by recording the changes in sweat response on the skin's surface. Some of the conditions which have been found to be responsive to biofeedback include phobias, anxiety, hypertension, bruxism, asthma, headaches, insomnia, circulatory problems like Raynaud's disease, muscle spasms, and temporomandibular joint syndrome (Stoyva & Budzynski, 1993). Chief advantages of biofeedback practice are (Greenberg, 1993):

- A greater control over the body and mind for the participant.

- An useful tool for psychologists to monitor bodily reactions to various stressors.

- An improvement in self-reliance of the participant in coping with stress.

A simple form of biofeedback can be obtained with the help of Biodots. Biodots are small circular, microencapsulated cholesteric liquid crystals measuring a broad thermal range. In simple terms they can be called miniature thermometers which provide a measurement of skin temperature. These are used as a very general indicator of skin temperature variance. Biodots are designed to be triggered at a temperature over 87°F. Biodots are a versatile and economical tool for persons trained to thermal responses. Biodots are an ideal, yet affordable, device for an introductory example to persons unfamiliar with the most general biofeedback techniques. A biodot can be applied to almost any part of the body. However, the most ideal location is the gentle dip of the juncture between the thumb and the forefinger (Figure 3-1). This site provides the participant with a constant view of the biodot for the purposes of monitoring color change. It is necessary to remember that Biodots are the simplist form of biofeedback, and therefore a great amount of "tradeoff" has to be done in terms of their accuracy. This means that Biodots may not be able to provide accurate color change for many of us, especially for those of us who typically have cold hands.

Biodots can be purchased from Biodot International, P.O. Box 2246, Indianapolis, IN 46206, (317) 637-5776. The various color changes which these biodots undergo are depicted in Table 3-1 on next page. For more information about Biofeedback the reader can contact the Biofeedback Society of America, Department of Psychiatry C 268, University of Colorado Medical Center, 4200 East Ninth Avenue, Denver, Colorado 80220.

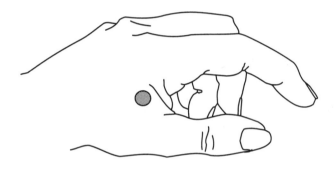

Figure 3-1 Site of Biodot Application

Table 3-1 Color changes on biodots and their interpretations

Color	Temperature	Interpretation
Black	87.5°F	• Indicative of highly tense moment • Normal initial color of the biodot
Amber	89.6°F	• Indicative of tense moment
Yellow	90.6°F	• Unsettled
Green	91.6°F	• Involved with the things going on around the person
Turquoise	92.6°F	• Starting to relax
Blue	93.6°F	• Calm
Violet	94.6°F	• Very relaxed

Progressive Muscle Relaxation

This method of relaxation was first described by a Chicago physician, Edmund Jacobson (1938, 1977). Jacobson designed this technique for hospital patients who were tense before surgery. He observed that these patients exhibited tenseness of small group muscles like the ones located in the back or neck and were thus unable to relax. Therefore, he taught these patients to first contract a set of muscles to experience tension and then gradually relax them. This process enabled the individual to discriminate between a relaxed and a tense state. This process was repeated for all other muscle groups throughout the body. The total skeletal muscles in the body number 1030 which are arranged in various groups. All these muscles can be relaxed by Progressive Muscle Relaxation practiced to cover one group of muscles at a time. This method has been found to be an excellent means by which to achieve relaxation of not only the body confined to skeletal muscles but also the mind and other internal organs. The primary feature of this method is the ability acquired by the practitioner to be able to selectively relax his or her muscle fibers on command, and this can then be done anytime (McGuigan, 1993). Jacobson spent over seven decades collecting data documenting effectiveness of progressive muscle relaxation in a scientific manner. This method has been shown to have application as a prophylactic method to reduce stress and tension. It also has applicability as a therapeutic measure. Its efficacy has been studied in nervous hypertension, acute insomnia with nervousness, anxiety neurosis, cardiac neurosis, chronic insomnia, cyclothymic depression, compulsive neurosis, hypochondria, fatigue states, nervous depression, and phobias. It has also been successfully applied to somatoform disorders like convulsive tic, esophageal spasm, mucus colitis, chronic colitis, arterial hypertension, and tension headaches (McGuinan, 1993). Bernstein and Carlson (1993) describe another shorter version of PMR known as "abbreviated progressive relaxation training" (APRT). Attempts to shorten the process of PMR were initiated by Joseph Wolpe (1958) whose method focused on relaxing several major muscle groups in seven sessions in contrast to Jacobson's program which focused on a single muscle group for several sessions before moving on to the next. This shorter version was further modified by Paul (1966) and formalized by Bernstein & Borkovec (1973). We have, in this workbook, described a modification of all these methods which also includes some ideas from Eastern thought. Let us now practice this method with the help of Worksheet 3.2.

Thoughts for Reflection 3.2 will help us to ponder on some of our life styles which if appropriately modified will provide us with greater relaxation and harmony in life.

Thoughts for Reflection 3.2

Think!

Before going to bed everyday, think . . .

- Did I work less, enough, or more? If less or more then contemplate why?

- Am I getting enough relaxation?

- Are there any lifestyles which I need to change?

Before beginning any new task or activity, think . . .

- Is it worth all the effort!

- Is there any other way to do it better?

- Will it be beneficial to self, family, and society?

- Can I do something else more beneficial in the same time?

Before owning any new object, think . . .

- Do I really need it?

- Is it worth owning?

- What will be the consequences if I own this object?

- What will be the consequences if I do <u>not</u> own this object?

- Will it bring happiness and peace to all?

<u>Note</u>. Based upon Eastern philosophy to obtain relaxation and peace.

* * * * * * * * * * * * * *

Worksheet 3.2
Progressive Muscle Relaxation

The method described is a slight modification of the classical approach as advocated by Edmund Jacobson (1938, 1977). The original method entails a longer time, greater practice, and is slightly more tedious. This method is a simplification of the classical approach and also incorporates the relaxation component of the physical exercises advocated in Simplified Kundalini Yoga (SKY) as described earlier (Maharishi, 1987).

Preparation
- Let us seek out a relatively quiet, distraction-free environment, where the practice can be continued for 30 minutes without any interruptions (telephone, doorbells, or people entering the room, etc.).
- We need to avoid any unnecessary movements (getting up, fidgeting, etc.) during this process.
- This technique is best practiced in a lying down supine position with arms placed alongside the body and eyes closed (Figure 3-2).

Figure 3-2 Position for Practicing Progressive Muscle Relaxation

Practice Session

We may want to record the following steps in our own voice on a tape recorder or we may ask another person to record these instructional steps for us. Some people prefer to just repeat the instructions mentally. This may require familiarity with these steps which can be accomplished by reading them two or three times.

Worksheet 3.2 Progressive Muscle Relaxation (Cont'd)

Step 1. Relaxation of the Arms (6 min.)

- Clench the left fist.
- Feel the tightness in the muscles of the left hand.
- Now, let go.
- Feel the relaxation in the muscles of the left hand.

- Clench the right fist.
- Feel the tightness in the muscles of the right hand.
- Now, let go.
- Feel the relaxation in the muscles of the right hand.

- Clench both fists together.
- Feel the tightness in the muscles of both hands.
- Now, let go.
- Feel the relaxation in the muscles of both hands.

- Bend the left arm at the elbow.
- Feel the tightness in the muscles of the left arm.
- Now, let go.
- Feel the relaxation in the muscles of the left arm.

- Bend the right arm at the elbow.
- Feel the tightness in the muscles of the right arm.
- Now, let go.
- Feel the relaxation in the muscles of the right arm.

- Bend both arms at the elbow.
- Feel the tightness in the muscles of both arms.
- Now, let go.
- Feel the relaxation in the muscles of the both arms.

Step 2. Relaxation of the Legs (7 min.)

- Bend the left foot upwards.
- Feel the tightness in the muscles of the left foot.
- Now, let go.
- Feel the relaxation in the muscles of the left foot.

- Bend the left foot downwards.
- Feel the tightness in the muscles of the left foot.
- Now, let go.
- Feel the relaxation in the muscles of the left foot.

Worksheet 3.2 Progressive Muscle Relaxation (Cont'd)

- Bend the right foot upwards.
- Feel the tightness in the muscles of the right foot.
- Now, let go.
- Feel the relaxation in the muscles of the right foot.

- Bend the right foot downwards.
- Feel the tightness in the muscles of the right foot.
- Now, let go.
- Feel the relaxation in the muscles of the right foot.

- Bend the left leg at the knee and tighten.
- Feel the tightness in the muscles of the left leg and thigh.
- Now, let go.
- Feel the relaxation in the muscles of the left leg and thigh.

- Bend the right leg at the knee and tighten.
- Feel the tightness in the muscles of the right leg and thigh.
- Now, let go.
- Feel the relaxation in the muscles of the right leg and thigh.

- Bend both legs at the knee and tighten.
- Feel the tightness in the muscles of both legs and thighs.
- Now, let go.
- Feel the relaxation in the muscles of both legs and thighs.

Step 3. Relaxation of the Face (5 min.)

- Place wrinkles on the forehead by lifting the eyebrows.
- Feel the tightness in the muscles of the forehead.
- Now, let go.
- Feel the relaxation in the muscles of the forehead.

- Frown by drooping the eyebrows.
- Feel the tightness in the surrounding muscles.
- Now, let go.
- Feel the relaxation in the surrounding muscles.

- Close both eyes tightly shut.
- Feel the tightness in the surrounding muscles.
- Now, let go.
- Feel the relaxation in the surrounding muscles.

Worksheet 3.2 Progressive Muscle Relaxation (Cont'd)

- Clench the jaw tightly.
- Feel the tightness in the surrounding muscles.
- Now, let go.
- Feel the relaxation in the surrounding muscles.

- Purse the lips tightly.
- Feel the tightness in the surrounding muscles.
- Now, let go.
- Feel the relaxation in the surrounding muscles.

Step 4. Relaxation of the Neck and Shoulders (6 min.)

- Bend the neck gently forwards.
- Feel the tightness in the muscles of the neck.
- Now, let go.
- Feel the relaxation in the muscles of the neck.

- Bend the neck gently backwards.
- Feel the tightness in the muscles of the neck.
- Now, let go.
- Feel the relaxation in the muscles of the neck.

- Bend the neck gently to the right.
- Feel the tightness in the muscles of the neck.
- Now, let go.
- Feel the relaxation in the muscles of the neck.

- Bend the neck gently to the left.
- Feel the tightness in the muscles of the neck.
- Now, let go.
- Feel the relaxation in the muscles of the neck.

- Shrug the left shoulder to touch the ear lobe.
- Feel the tightness in the muscles of the left shoulder.
- Now, let go.
- Feel the relaxation in the muscles of the left shoulder.

- Shrug the right shoulder to touch the ear lobe.
- Feel the tightness in the muscles of the right shoulder.
- Now, let go.
- Feel the relaxation in the muscles of the right shoulder.

Worksheet 3.2 Progressive Muscle Relaxation (Cont'd)

Step 5. Relaxation of the Trunk (2 min.)

- Inhale deeply to tighten the chest muscles.
- Feel the tightness in the muscles of the chest.
- Now, let go.
- Feel the relaxation in the muscles of the chest.

- Exhale with force to tighten the abdominal muscles.
- Feel the tightness in the muscles of the abdomen.
- Now, let go.
- Feel the relaxation in the muscles of the abdomen.

Step 6. Relaxation of the Whole Body (4 min.)
 [Let us give ourselves the following Autosuggestions (see
 Thoughts for Reflection 3.3 which follows)]

- My feet are relaxed and healthy.
- My ankles are relaxed and healthy.
- My legs are relaxed and healthy.
- My knees are relaxed and healthy.
- My thighs are relaxed and healthy.
- My hips and pelvis are relaxed and healthy.
- My abdomen and parts within are relaxed and healthy.
- My chest and parts within are relaxed and healthy.
- My shoulders are relaxed and healthy.
- My arms are relaxed and healthy.
- My elbows are relaxed and healthy.
- My forearms are relaxed and healthy.
- My wrists are relaxed and healthy.
- My hands are relaxed and healthy.
- My neck is relaxed and healthy.
- My face is relaxed and healthy.
- My mind is relaxed and healthy.

FEEDBACK ON WORKSHEET 3.2

   Progressive Muscle Relaxation is an excellent relaxing method with
evidence to support its application as both prophylactic and therapeutic
measure (Jacobson, 1938, 1977; McGuigan, 1993). The key to complete success
lies in daily regular practice.

Thoughts for Reflection 3.3

Autosuggestions

Autosuggestions or talking with oneself is a powerful means to develop self-confidence and build healthy lifestyles. Dr. Emile Coupe, a French psychotherapist, was the first to come up with the best well-known phrase for autosuggestion —"Day by day in every way, I am getting better and better" (Patel, 1993). Reflect upon the following ideas for possible autosuggestions within the context of bringing relaxation in our life. After thinking through this list, we may like to come up with a personal list of autosuggestions for ourselves. These autosuggestions can be repeated to ourselves during our free time or routinely during morning and evening or coupled with practice of other relaxation methods.

- I am happy, healthy, and relaxed.

- I am in harmony with my surroundings.

- I work efficiently and sufficiently.

- I enjoy complete peace of mind.

- My sleep is sound, refreshing and relaxing.

- My relationship with self and others is cordial.

- I stay calm and relaxed even in potentially tense situations.

- All the organs and organ systems in my body are working and relaxing optimally.

Autogenic Training

Autogenic training owes its origin to the work by a German neurologist, Johannes Heinrich Schultz. He described it as a self-hypnotic procedure (Schultz, 1932). Autogenic therapy is a derivative of hypnosis and has been also described as "psychophysiological self control therapy" (Pikoff, 1984).

Since this technique originated in Germany, it became and remains quite popular in European countries and Japan. This technique became known in North America when one of Schultz's followers, Wolfgang Luthe, a physician, emigrated to Canada and translated much of this work in English. There is ample evidence that it is an useful stress-reducing technique. It is also useful as a curative approach in dealing with anxiety and related disorders (Luthe, 1970). The term "autogenic" is derived from Greek words *autos* meaning self, and *genos* meaning origin. Therefore, in this technique basically, the self-regulation and self-healing powers of the mind are channelized in a positive manner. The practitioner of autogenic training concentrates on his or her body sensations in a passive manner without directly or volitionally bringing about any change (Linden, 1993). The key sensations on which the mind is focused include those of heaviness and warmth. Focusing on these sensations provides the body with a feeling of relaxation because these sensations are normally associated with the relaxation process. Let us now practice a slightly modified version of this technique which incorporates the key principles with the help of Worksheet 3.3.

Visual Imagery

Visual Imagery is mental visualization with the help of imagination. It is an important component of all relaxation procedures. It is somewhat akin to dreaming. It has been used both in the East as well as in the West. It is based on the principle that whatever we think and imagine has a profound and deep impact on our body. The key emphasis of visual imagery lies in enhancing an individual's innate capacity to attain and maintain health (Miller & Lueth, 1978). This technique can be used to accomplish effective results in almost all spheres of life. For example, in the training of athletes and sportspersons, visual imagery is extensively utilized. Regular visual imagery training provides the athletes to mentally visualize beforehand various situations (like performing in front of large crowds, winning an event, etc.) and techniques (like swinging a bat, shooting baskets, etc.). Regular practice of visual imagery has been shown to improve performance, especially in tournaments and competitions.

Within the context of relaxation, imagining relaxing scenes and images is a very useful way to bring about relaxation. Visual imagery can also be used to overcome barriers which hinder effective relaxation by mentally visualizing them beforehand. Worksheet 3.4 helps us to practice visual imagery for relaxation.

Thoughts for Reflection 3.3 presented earlier provided us with some ideas for autosuggestions or self talk which can enhance the benefits of relaxation.

Worksheet 3.3
Autogenic Training

The following steps are a slight modification of the conventional autogenic training method developed by Schultz (1932). If practiced regularly, this method can reduce stress and provide effective relaxation.

Preparation

Let us choose a quiet and comfortable place. We may practice this method either in a sitting position or in a lying down position. Let us choose a position in which we are comfortable. Let us close our eyes while practicing this technique. We may repeat the suggestions in the following steps either mentally or record them on a tape recorder and listen to the tape whenever we practice autogenic training.

<u>Step 1</u>.   **Heaviness of the arms (2 min)**

- My right arm, forearm and hand are getting heavy.
- I am feeling heaviness in my right arm, forearm and hand.
- My left arm, forearm and hand are getting heavy.
- I am feeling heaviness in my left arm, forearm and hand.

<u>Step 2</u>.   **Heaviness of the legs (2 min)**

- My right thigh, leg and foot are getting heavy.
- I am feeling heaviness in my right thigh, leg and foot.
- My left thigh, leg and foot are getting heavy.
- I am feeling heaviness in my left thigh, leg and foot.

<u>Step 3</u>.   **Warmth in the arms (2 min)**

- My right arm, forearm and hand are getting warm.
- I am feeling warmth in my right arm, forearm and hand.
- My left arm, forearm, and hand are getting warm.
- I am feeling warmth in my left arm, forearm and hand.

Worksheet 3.3 Autogenic Training (Cont'd)

<u>Step 4.</u>   **Warmth in the legs (2 min)**

- My right thigh, leg and foot are getting warm.
- I am feeling warmth in my right thigh, leg and foot.
- My left thigh, leg and foot are getting warm.
- I am feeling warmth in my left thigh, leg and foot.

<u>Step 5.</u>   **Strength of the heart (2 min)**

- My heart beats are regular and steady.
- My heart is strong and healthy.
- I am feeling strength in my heart.

<u>Step 6.</u>   **Strength of breathing (2 min)**

- My breathing is regular and steady.
- My lungs are strong and healthy.
- My respiratory tract is clear and healthy.
- I am feeling strength in my lungs and respiratory tract.

<u>Step 7.</u>   **Strength of all visceral organs (2 min)**

- All my internal organs are healthy.
- I am feeling strength in all my internal organs.

<u>Step 8.</u>   **Coolness of the forehead (2 min)**

- My forehead is cool and relaxed.

<u>Step 9.</u>   **Finishing (1 min)**

- My body and mind are completely relaxed and rested.

(Gradually open your eyes and get up)

* * * * * * * * * * * * * *

Worksheet 3.4
Visual Imagery

Let us solicit a quiet and comfortable place. Let us leave aside all our other activities for at least half an hour. If possible, the place should not have any sources of possible distraction like telephone, small children playing and so on. We may choose to lie down or sit.

- Let us close our eyes.

- Let us recollect the last time when we were extremely happy. It may be with someone, it may be that we had been somewhere, it may be that we got something. Whatever made us happy, let us mentally imagine that scene.

- Let us forget about everything else and just get engrossed in imagining that happy moment and scene.

- Let us remain with this feeling mentally for at least ten minutes.

- Now let us imagine any event which we may not have experienced but which we believe will make us happy.

- Let us mentally enjoy the feeling of being in that event.

- Let us be with this feeling for at least ten minutes.

- Now we can open our eyes and feel the relaxation and recharging of the system which has taken place.

* * * * * * * * * * * * * *

Stress Management Principle # 3

Let us make relaxation a part of life.

Summary Points

- Relaxation is essential for normal functioning of all living beings. Relaxation techniques are the core of all stress management programs.

- Natural process of relaxation is sleep. Sleep conserves and restores energy.

- Sleep has two phases Rapid Eye Movement (REM) and Non Rapid Eye Movement (Non REM). During Non REM phase the mind reaches subtler frequencies as recorded on an electroencephalogram (EEG).

- Some of the techniques for relaxation are Yoga, Meditation, Yogic Breathing or "*Pranayama*," Biofeedback, Progressive Muscle Relaxation (PMR), Autogenic Training (AT), and Visual Imagery.

- Yoga is a systematic application of the mind and body to achieve overall harmony and peace.

- Some systems of Yoga popular in the West include Transcendental Meditation (TM), *Kriya Yoga,* and *Simplified Kundalini Yoga.*

- Biofeedback utilizes instruments to provide awareness about bodily functions which may then be brought under voluntary control.

- Progressive Muscle Relaxation (PMR) was first described by Edmund Jacobson. It is an effective means of achieving relaxation.

- Autogenic Training was first described by J. H. Schultz and utilizes the self-regulation and self-healing processes of the mind to achieve relaxation.

- Visual Imagery or mental visualization with the help of imagination is an important component of all relaxation procedures.

References and Further Readings

Bernstein, D. A., & Borkovec, T. D. (1973). Progressive relaxation training: A manual for the helping professions. Champaign, IL: Research Press.

Bernstein, D. A., & Carlson, C. R. (1993). Progressive relaxation: Abbreviated methods. In P. M. Lehrer & R. L. Woolfolk (Eds.), Principles and practice of stress management. (2nd ed.), (pp. 53-88). New York, NY: The Guilford Press.

Brown, B. (1974). New mind, new body, biofeedback: New directions for the mind. New York, NY: Harper & Row.

Fuller, G.D. (1977). Biofeedback: Methods and procedures in clinical practice. San Francisco, CA: Biofeedback Press.

Kalat, J.W. (1988). Biological psychology. (3rd ed). New York, NY: Wadsworth Publishing Company.

Karlins, M., & Andrews, L.W. (1972). Biofeedback: Turning on the powers of your mind. New York, NY: J.B. Lippincott.

Kumar, C. S. C. (1993, August 29). What is TM? The Week, 10 -15.

Linden, W. (1993). The autogenic training method of J. H. Schultz. In P. M. Lehrer & R. L. Woolfolk (Eds.), Principles and practice of stress management. (2nd ed.), (pp. 53-88). New York, NY: The Guilford Press.

Luthe, W. (1970). Autogenic therapy: Research and theory. Vol. 4. New York, NY: Grune & Stratton.

Maharishi, Y.V. (1986). Karma yoga the holistic unity. Madras, India: Vethathiri Publications.

Maharishi, Y. V. (1987). Simplified physical exercises. Erode, India: Vethathiri Publications.

Maharishi, Y.V. (1989). Yoga for modern age. Madras, India: Vethathiri Publications.

McGuigan, F.J. (1993). Progressive relaxation: origins, principles, and clinical applications. In P. M. Lehrer & R. L. Woolfolk (Eds.), Principles & Practice of Stress Management. (2nd ed.), (pp. 17-52). New York, NY: The Guilford Press.

Miller, E.E., & Lueth, D. (1978). Self imagery. Creating your own good health. Berkeley, CA: Celestial Arts.

References and Further Readings (Cont'd)

Naranjo, C., & Ornstein, R.E. (1971). On the psychology of meditation. New York, NY: Viking.

Patel C. (1993). Yoga based therapy. In P. M. Lehrer & R. L. Woolfolk (Eds.), Principles and Practice of Stress Management. (2nd ed.), (pp. 89-137). New York, NY: The Guilford Press.

Paul, G. L. (1966). Insight versus desensitization in psychotherapy. Stanford, CA: Stanford University Press.

Pikoff, H. (1984). A critical review of autogenic training in America. Clinical Psychology Review, 4, 619-639.

Schultz, J. H. (1932). Das Autogene Training-Konzentrative Selbstentspannung. [German]. Leipzig, Germany: Thieme.

Shapiro, C. M., & Flanigan, M.J. (1993). Function of sleep, British Medical Journal, 306, 383-385.

Singh, K. (1983). Hinduism. In Religions of India. New Delhi, India: Clarion Books.

Stoyva, J. M. & Budzynski, T.H. (1993). Biofeedback methods in the treatment of anxiety and stress disorders. In P. M. Lehrer & R. L. Woolfolk (Eds.), Principles & Practice of Stress Management. (2nd Ed.), (pp. 263-300). New York, NY: The Guilford Press.

Vasu, R. B. S. C. (1915). An introduction to the yoga philosophy. Allahabad, India: The Panini Office.

Wolpe, J. (1958). Psychotherapy by reciprocal inhibition. Stanford, CA: Stanford University   Press.

Yogananda, P. (1946). Autobiography of a yogi. Los Angeles, CA: Self-Realization Fellowship.

CHAPTER 4

EFFECTIVE COMMUNICATION

No man Speaks . . .

No man speaks concerning another,
even suppose it be in his praise,
if he thinks he does not hear him,
exactly as he would,
if he thought he was within hearing.

Samuel Johnson

What Is Communication?

We spend nearly 70 percent of our waking hours communicating — reading, writing, speaking, and listening (Robbins, 1991). If this communication becomes defective or faulty, it often leads to stress. Therefore, it is important for us to become effective communicators.

Before we proceed any further, let us first define the term communication. One of the definitions which will come to our minds will be "transfer of meaning." Is communication just "transfer of meaning?" Perhaps it is more than just the transfer of meaning from one person to another. The important aspect in communication is the ability for the message to be understood — unless the meaning is understood, communication will remain incomplete and ineffective. These two aspects — transference and understanding of meaning — are extremely complex in their dimensions. Since we communicate very often, we seldom realize and appreciate the complexities involved.

Today the English language has more than 600,000 words available. According to linguists, an average educated adult uses about 2000 of these words in daily conversation. But the problem is that out of these words, 500 of the words most frequently used have more than 14,000 dictionary definitions (Burke, Hall, & Hawley, 1986). And each one of us has his or her unique perspective in using and interpreting these words. More often than not this multiplicity leads to problematic communication. Furthermore, language is only a small tool which is used for communicating. A significant amount of communication occurs by our non-verbal gestures, tone of voice, and so on.

The Communication Process

Communication was first described as a process by Berlo (1960). This model is one of the most popular ones. It is also known as the SMCR Model (Sender, Message, Channel, Receiver). The message to be conveyed passes between the sender (the source) and the receiver. The message is converted to a symbolic form (encoded) and is passed by way of some channel (medium) to the receiver who retranslates (decodes) the message initiated by the sender. In this way transference of meaning from one person to another results.

Figure 4-1 Berlo's SMCR Model of Communication

Let us try to understand what goes into each of these components. The **sender** initiates communication by **encoding** or converting a communication message to symbolic form. This process is influenced by the following factors:

- Knowledge or information about the message.

- Skills like writing, speaking, etc.

- Attitudes which are constant feelings directed toward an object (person, situation, or an idea) and have an evaluative dimension (Green & Kreuter, 1991; Mucchielli, 1970).

- Beliefs which are convictions that a phenomenon or object is true or real (Rokeach, 1970).

- Values or cultural intergenerational perspectives (Rokeach, 1970).

The **message** is the actual physical product from the sender encoding it. For example, when we speak, the speech is the message; when we write, the writing is the message; when we gesture, the body movements are the message, and so on.

The medium through which a communication message travels is the **channel**. Myers & Nance (1991) in <u>The Upset Book</u> have identified seven channels of communication, namely:

1. Language ("what" part of the message)

2. Manner (how we express the message or say it vocally)

3. Body language (how we express the message visually through our body movements)

4. Feelings (emotions)

5. Symbolic communication (for example; dress, hairstyle, appearance, and so on)

6. Territory (personal: physiological and psychological)

7. Behavior (intentional and not so intentional actions)

The **receiver** is the object to whom the message is directed. But before the message can be received, the symbols in it must be translated into a form that can be deciphered. This is the **decoding** and is influenced by similar factors as discussed in encoding earlier. The final link in the communication process is a **feedback loop** which puts the message back into the system as a check against misunderstandings. All of these seven components mentioned above are subject to possible distortion and can thereby contribute to the cause of stress.

Now let us assess ourselves as to how well we communicate through Worksheet 4.1. Worksheet 4.2 will help us identify our communication process in various situations and will provide feedback on ways to improve upon communication.

Worksheet 4.1
Communication Assessment

This is a self-assessment tool which enhances our awareness on various attributes of effective communication and has no right or wrong answers. It can also be used for gathering feedback from others about us as communicators. So we can ask our spouse, a family member, friend, colleague, or someone who knows us to fill out this worksheet for us.

How would we rate ourselves (or the person whom we are assessing) on the following items?

Excellent = 5, Very good = 4, Satisfactory = 3, Poor = 2, Very Poor = 1:

While communicating . . .

Rating Scale

1.	I am concise and to the point.	5	4	3	2	1
2.	I express myself clearly.	5	4	3	2	1
3.	I modulate the tone of my voice to convey precise meaning.	5	4	3	2	1
4.	I use appropriate body gestures and facial expressions.	5	4	3	2	1
5.	I am forceful and definite rather than hesitant and apologetic.	5	4	3	2	1
6.	I summarize the key points.	5	4	3	2	1
7.	I do not talk in round about ways.	5	4	3	2	1
8.	I am specific and give examples to make my points clear.	5	4	3	2	1
9.	I let others know in unambiguous terms when I do not follow them.	5	4	3	2	1
10.	I often ask others if they have followed me.	5	4	3	2	1

Worksheet 4.1 Communication Assessment (Cont'd)

11. I help others participate in the discussion.	5	4	3	2	1
12. I listen actively.	5	4	3	2	1
13. I keep my feelings under check.	5	4	3	2	1
14. I do not react to the feelings of others.	5	4	3	2	1
15. I listen to understand rather than prepare for the next remark.	5	4	3	2	1
16. I avoid using jargon and use simple language.	5	4	3	2	1
17. I give equal respect to others as communicators.	5	4	3	2	1
18. I try to see the other person's point of view.	5	4	3	2	1
19. I do not divert myself while communicating.	5	4	3	2	1
20. I am able to withstand silence.	5	4	3	2	1

FEEDBACK ON WORKSHEET 4.1

Having rated yourself and also having elicited feedback from others you will now be quite clear about your strengths and limitations. Try to build further on your strengths (categories in which you have rated excellent and very good). Also try to overcome your limitations (categories in which you have rated yourself or have been rated as satisfactory, poor, or very poor).

* * * * * * * * * * * * * * *

Worksheet 4.2
Communication in Various Situations

This worksheet provides us with certain situations. Let us circle the answer that best describes what we would do in each situation.

1. I have an important appointment in the next one-half hour and my best friend arrives. Would I . . .
    a. ask my spouse to handle the situation and leave from the back door
    b. exchange pleasantries and excuse myself politely
    c. cancel the appointment
    d. hurriedly leave

2. I need to imagine myself to be working in a middle management position. The head of the organization invites me for lunch. When I return, I sense that my department head is curious.
Would I . . .
    a. ignore him or her
    b. give a detailed description
    c. mention the meeting casually — as though nothing has happened
    d. fabricate a story

3. My boyfriend (or girlfriend) is not able to keep a date with me. Would I . . .
    a. act as if nothing has happened
    b. ask him or her the reasons
    c. wait for his or her explanations
    d. walk out on him or her

4. My spouse tells me a juicy story about the neighbor's daughter which he or she has heard from somewhere. Would I say . . .
    a. "I don't want to hear any of this."
    b. "I am not interested."
    c. "What happened next?"
    d. "How does it concern us?"

Worksheet 4.2 Communication in Various Situations (Cont'd)

5. I had to stay late at the office completing pending work. I returned home
    and am tired. My spouse inquires the reason for my coming in late. Do I . . .
    a. tell him or her to mind their own business
    b. explain the reason clearly
    c. ignore him or her
    d. change the topic of conversation

6. My supervisor, in a staff meeting, makes an inaccurate statement. Would I . . .
    a. correct my supervisor on the spot
    b. correct my supervisor later away from the meeting
    c. ask a clarifying question at the meeting and discuss the matter later
    d. tell other staff members how foolish my supervisor is

7. I am at a party, and someone introduces me to a person of different ethnic
    orientation. After initiating conversation, I am unable to understand the
    other person. Would I . . .
    a. politely excuse yourself
    b. ask the person for repeated clarifications
    c. nod in agreement
    d. form an opinion about his/her poor communication skills

8. A friend calls me on the phone and invites me to a sports event. I have
    made other plans with another person but would very much like to go.
    Would I . . .
    a. call my other friend and cancel the appointment so I can go to the
       sports event
    b. ask my friend if the other person can come along to the sports event
    c. persuade my friend to cancel going to the sports event and join me
    d. cancel both engagements and stay at home

9. I enter into a meeting and find that all the members have burst into
    laughter. Would I . . .
    a. assume that they are laughing at me and leave the meeting
    b. assume that they are laughing at me and speak against their
       inappropriate behavior
    c. laugh with them and later ask the reason for laughing
    d. sit quietly and ask nothing

10. I give my teenage son or daughter a specific time to be home. He or she
    openly defies my directive by coming home very late. Would I . . .
    a. reprimand him or her and decide not to talk about it again
    b. discuss the matter openly the next day
    c. blame my spouse for spoiling the teenager
    d. call up the other parents and complain

FEEDBACK ON WORKSHEET 4.2

Most appropriate responses which would help us prevent undue stress from occurring in our life because of improper communication are as follows:

1. b   This would prevent any miscommunication and misunderstanding to occur.

2. b   Our loyalty lies to our immediate supervisor. If we fabricate or ignore or do not tell enough, it will sow the seeds of mistrust and create stress later.

3. b   An open discussion would help us understand his or her problem and avoid undue stress.

4. d   We need to avoid gossip to float around unless it concerns us and then try to find the facts. In this way miscommunication and associated problems leading to stress can be avoided.

5. b   This would prevent any miscommunication and misunderstanding to occur.

6. c   Asking a clarification question at the time of the discussion will help our supervisor to correct himself or herself, if he or she has made the statement out of oversight. If not, discussion at a later time will help clarify our point of view without embarrassing our supervisor.

7. b   Repeated clarifications will help us gain an understanding of what the other person is trying to communicate and lessen stress for both of us.

8. b   Accomplishing our goals without hurting the feelings of others are a part of assertiveness and effectively communicating. Being up front about our position will help to reduce stress.

9. c   Laughing with people, even if we are being laughed at, will reduce undue discomfort to us. Soliciting clarification later on will help us understand the actual reason.

10. b   An open discussion about the matter will help both of us to clarify our viewpoints and reach mutual understanding to reduce family stress.

The worksheet above helps us to appreciate the importance of straightforwardness and assertiveness in our communication with others in order to reduce stress.

* * * * * * * * * * * * * *

Assertiveness

Another important aspect of communication is the ability to say "no," if you want to say "no," without feeling guilty. This is known as being assertive. Assertiveness has been defined as "expressing personal rights and feelings" (Lazarus, 1966; Wolpe, 1958). In another way it can be defined as expressing oneself, satisfying one's personal needs, feeling good about this, and not hurting others in the process (Greenberg, 1993). Worksheet 4.3 on Assessing Assertive Behavior will help us to gain insight into passive, assertive, and aggressive behaviors when communicating with others.

 Research shows that nearly everybody can be assertive in some situations while in others the same person will be ineffectual. The goal therefore is to increase the number and variety of situations in which assertive behavior is possible. This decreases the events in which a passive behavior or a hostile blowup will occur.

Assertiveness is not the same as aggressiveness. One can differentiate between the two by asking three simple questions:

1.   Am I violating someone else's rights?

2.   Do others react to me by getting angry or upset?

3.   Do I intend to be malicious or do I intend to be fair to all concerned?

Aggressiveness means seeking to dominate or to get your own way at the expense of others. This tendency should be curbed as far as possible and replaced with assertiveness. Let us practice to be more assertive as shown in Worksheet 4.4.

Thoughts for Reflection 4.1

A Bill of Assertive Rights

1. You have the right to judge your own behavior, thoughts, and emotions, and to take responsibility for their initiation and consequences upon yourself.

2. You have the right to offer no reasons or excuses for justifying your behavior.

3. You have the right to judge if you are responsible for finding solutions to other people's problems.

4. You have the right to change your mind.

5. You have the right to make mistakes — and be responsible for them.

6. You have the right to say, " I don't know."

7. You have the right to be independent of the goodwill of others before coping with them.

8. You have the right to be illogical in making decisions.

9. You have the right to say, "I don't understand."

10. You have the right to say, "I don't care."

* * * * * * * * * * * * * *

Worksheet 4.3
Assessing Assertive Behavior

To determine our general pattern of behavior, let us indicate how characteristic or descriptive each of the following statements is of us by using the code that follows:

+3 = very characteristic of me, extremely descriptive
+2 = rather characteristic of me, quite descriptive
+1 = somewhat characteristic of me, slightly descriptive
-1 = somewhat uncharacteristic of me, slightly nondescriptive
-2 = rather uncharacteristic of me, quite nondescriptive
-3 = very uncharacteristic of me, extremely nondescriptive

____   1.   Most people seem to be more aggressive and assertive than I am.

____   2.   I have hesitated to make or accept dates because of "shyness."

____   3.   When the food served at a restaurant is not done to my satisfaction, I complain about it to the waiter or waitress.

____   4.   I am careful to avoid hurting other people's feelings, even when I feel that I have been injured.

____   5.   If a salesperson has gone to considerable trouble to show me merchandise that is not quite suitable, I have a difficult time in saying no.

____   6.   When I am asked to do something, I insist upon knowing why.

____   7.   There are times when I look for a good, vigorous argument.

____   8.   I strive to get ahead as well as most people in my position.

____   9.   To be honest, people often take advantage of me.

____   10.   I enjoy starting conversations with new acquaintances and strangers.

____   11.   I often don't know what to say to attractive persons of the opposite sex.

____   12.   I will hesitate to make phone calls to business establishments and institutions.

Worksheet 4.3 Assessing Assertive Behavior (Cont'd)

____ 13.   I would rather apply for a job or for admission to a college by writing letters than by going through with personal interviews.

____ 14.   I find it embarrassing to return merchandise.

____ 15.   If a close and respected relative were annoying me, I would smother my feeling rather than express my annoyance.

____ 16.   I have avoided asking questions for fear of sounding stupid.

____ 17.   During an argument I am sometimes afraid that I will get so upset that I will shake all over.

____ 18.   If a famed and respected lecturer makes a statement that I think is incorrect, I will have the audience hear my point of view.

____ 19.   I avoid arguing over prices with clerks and sales people.

____ 20.   When I have done something important or worthwhile, I manage to let others know about it.

____ 21.   I am open and frank about my feelings.

____ 22.   If someone has been spreading false and bad stories about me, I see him or her as soon as possible to "have a talk" about it.

____ 23.   I often have a hard time saying no.

____ 24.   I tend to bottle up my emotions rather than make a scene.

____ 25.   I complain about poor service in a restaurant and elsewhere.

____ 26.   When I am given a compliment, I sometimes just don't know what to say.

____ 27.   If a couple near me in a theater or at a lecture were conversing rather loudly, I would ask them to be quiet or to take their conversation elsewhere.

____ 28.   Anyone attempting to push ahead of me in a line is in for a good battle.

____ 29.   I am quick to express an opinion.

____ 30.   There are times when I just can't say anything.

Note. From "A 30 item schedule for assessing assertive behavior" by S.A. Rathus, 1973, Behavior Therapy, 4, 398-406. Copyright 1973 by Academic Press. Reprinted by permission.

FEEDBACK ON WORKSHEET 4.3

To score this scale, let us first change (reverse) the signs (+ or -) for our scores on items 1, 2, 4, 5, 9, 11, 12, 13, 14, 15, 16, 17, 19, 23, 24, 26, and 30. Now let us total the plus (+) items, total the minus (-) items, and subtract the minus total from the plus total to obtain our score. This score can range from -90 through 0 to +90. The higher the score (closer to 90) the more assertively we usually behave. The lower the score (closer to -90) the more nonassertive is our typical behavior. This particular scale does not measure aggressiveness.

* * * * * * * * * * * * * *

Worksheet 4.4
Five Steps to Becoming Assertive

The following is a stepwise process to become more assertive. Let us find a quiet place to work on this worksheet and proceed as directed.

Step 1. Identification of an Environmental Situation

We need to identify an environmental situation on which we want feedback. It may be our work situation or it may be our personal life or something else. Let us write it down in the following space:

_____

_____

Step 2. Behavior Style Classification

Let us identify and encircle our style of interpersonal behavior as

- Passive: avoids problems, allows manipulation by others, gives up one's rights, and lacks self-confidence. This type of behavior is stress-producing.

- Assertive: faces problems, gains respect from others by letting them know one's opinions, claims rights, and has self-confidence. This type of behavior is least stress-producing.

- Aggressive: attacks the other person, takes advantage of people, disregards the rights of others, and is often hostile. This type of behavior is most stress-producing.

Reasons:

_____

_____

_____

Worksheet 4.4 Five Steps to Becoming Assertive (Cont'd)

Step 3. Person Identification.

All situations involve some persons. Let us identify the persons with whom you would like to be more assertive. Let us list them below:

_____

_____

_____

_____

Step 4. Script Writing.

Let us write a script for changing our actions and reactions in order to become more assertive with these people.

a. Let us identify our rights and feelings — define our goal.

_____

_____

_____

_____

b. Let us describe our feelings by using "I" statements. For example, "I like to . . ." "I shall . . ."

_____

_____

_____

_____

Worksheet 4.4 Five Steps to Becoming Assertive (Cont'd)

<u>Step 5</u>. <u>Discussion Session</u>

Let us discuss with the person with whom we would like to be more assertive using the following checklist:

- Arrange a time and place for discussion.

- Concisely <u>define</u> the problem.

- <u>Describe</u> our feelings in "I" messages.

- Make our <u>request</u> in a brief sentence or two.

- <u>Reinforce</u> the other person's thinking by stating positive consequences of cooperation and if necessary negative consequences for failure to cooperate.

- Use of assertive <u>body language</u> like direct eye contact, erect body posture, clarity of speech.

- Avoiding manipulation.

- Be willing to compromise if it is essential.

* * * * * * * * * * * * * * *

Worksheets 4.3 and 4.4 have provided us with an insight as to whether or not we are assertive. Some characteristics of an assertive person include:

- direct eye contact

- appropriate use of hand movements

- firm posture

- steady utilization of voice

- use of "I" statements

- speech meanings conveyed in short sentences

- feedback pauses

A person exhibiting assertiveness always uses direct eye contact while talking by looking the other person in the eye while communicating. An assertive person utilizes appropriate hand movements while communicating, being careful not to cause discomfort or invade the other person's space. An assertive person engages in a firm posture, not too stiff, yet not too relaxed, which maintains an appropriate distance in which both parties are comfortable. An assertive person uses a steady, consistent voice, keeping emotion to a minimum. One of the key characteristics of an assertive person is the use of "I" statements when speaking which demonstrates to others that an assertive person owns his or her behavior and is responsible for any action thereof. An assertive person uses short sentences expressing clarity and brevity in thought. Finally, an assertive person often pauses to obtain feedback from others which is vital for effective communication to take place. Thoughts for Reflection 4.2 provide us with some ideas for becoming assertive and Thoughts for Reflection 4.3 describe Nine Types of Assertive Responses.

Thoughts for Reflection 4.2

Assertive Communication Techniques

- Broken Record. A systematic communication skill in which one is persistent and keeps saying what one wants over and over again without getting angry, irritated or loud. By practicing to speak like a broken record, we learn to be persistent and to stick to the point of discussion and to continue to say what we want. This technique helps us to ignore all side issues brought up by the other party.

- Workable Compromise. A technique to utilize with an equally assertive person to work out a compromise. A workable compromise is one in which our self-respect is not in question.

- Free Information. A listening skill in which we evaluate and then follow up on the free information that people offer about themselves. It accomplishes two things. It makes it easier for us to converse comfortably with people and it is assertively prompting to others to speak easily and freely with us.

- Self-Disclosure. Assertively disclosing information about ourselves. How we think, feel and react to the other person's free information — permits social communication to flow both ways. It goes hand in hand with free information because in order to elicit more information, we must be willing for self-disclosure.

- Fogging. A technique to assertively cope with manipulative criticism, in which we do not deny any of the criticism, we do not get defensive and we do not attack with criticism of our own. We send up a fog bank. It is persistent. It cannot be clearly seen through. It offers no resistance to penetration. It does not fight back and has no hard striking surfaces. Fogging permits us to cope by offering no resistance or hard psychological striking surfaces to critical statements thrown at us.

- Negative Assertion. A technique in which we cope with criticism or with our own errors and faults by openly acknowledging them. This technique is to be used only in social conflicts and not physical or legal ones.

- Negative Inquiry. An assertive, nondefensive response that is noncritical of the other person and prompts that person to make further critical statements to examine his or her own structure of right and wrong which he or she is using in certain situations, e.g. "I don't understand. What makes you think educators are stupid?"

Note. From Stress Stoppers: Managing Stress Effectively (p. 25) by P.R. Kovacek, 1981, Detroit, MI: Henry Ford Hospital. Material under public domain.

Thoughts for Reflection 4.3

Nine Types of Assertive Responses

1. Assertive Talk: Do not let others take advantage of you. Expect to be treated with fairness and justice. Example: "I was here first," "Please turn down the radio," I've been waiting here for half an hour," and "This steak is well-done and I ordered it medium-rare."

2. Feeling Talk: Express your likes and dislikes spontaneously. Be open and frank about your feelings. Do not bottle up emotions, but don't let emotions control you. Examples: "What a marvelous shirt!" "How great you look!" "I hate this cold," "I'm tired as hell," "Since you ask, I do prefer you in another type of outfit."

3. Greeting Talk: Be outgoing and friendly with people whom you would like to know better. Do not avoid people because of shyness, because you do not know what to say. Smile brightly at people. Look and sound pleased to see them. Examples: "Hi, how are you?" "Hello, I haven't seen you in months," "What are you doing with yourself these days?" "How do you like working at _____?" "Taking any good courses?" "What's been happening with so and so?"

4. Disagreeing Passively and Actively: When you disagree with someone, do not feign agreement for the sake of "keeping the peace" by smiling, nodding, or paying close attention. Change the topic. Look away. Disagree actively when you are sure of your ground. Use fogging with manipulative criticizers.

5. Asking Why: When you are asked to do something that does not sound reasonable or enjoyable by a person in power or authority, ask why you should do it. You are an adult and should not accept authority alone. Ask for reasonable explanations from teachers, relatives and other authority figures. Have it understood that you will live up to voluntary commitments and be open to reasonable suggestions, but that you cannot comply with unreasonable orders.

6. Talking about Oneself: When you have done something worthwhile or interesting, let others know about it. Let people know how you feel about things. Relate your experiences. Do not monopolize conversations, but do not be afraid to bring them around to yourself when it is appropriate.

7. Agreeing with Compliments: Do not depreciate yourself or become flustered when someone compliments you with sincerity. At the very least, offer an equally sincere "Thank you." Or reward the complimenter by saying, "That's an awfully nice thing to say. I appreciate it."

Thoughts for Reflection 4.3

Nine Types of Assertive Responses (Cont'd)

8. <u>Avoid Trying Justification of Opinions</u>: Be reasonable in discussions, but when someone goes out of his/her way to dominate a social interaction by taking issue with any comments you offer, use a technique like "broken record."

9. <u>Looking People in the Eye</u>: Do not avoid the gaze of others. When you argue, express an opinion , or greet a person, look him or her directly in the eye.

<u>Note</u>. Adapted from <u>Behavior Research & Therapy. II,</u> S.A. Rathus, "Instigation of assertive behavior through video tape mediated assertive models and directed practice," pp. 57-65. Copyright © 1973 with kind permission from Elsevier Science Ltd., The Boulevard, Langford Lane, Kidlington, OX5 1GB, UK.

Behavioral Styles

Now that we have practiced assertiveness, let us focus our attention on another important aspect of communication, that is, on how we behave. All of us have developed certain behavioral patterns — distinct ways of thinking, feeling, and acting. The central core of these patterns tends to remain stable because it reflects our individual identities. However, the demands of the world around us (namely, personal, family, school, and work) often require different responses which evolve into a consistent behavioral style (Carlson Learning Company, 1993). One of the tools to explain behavioral styles is the Personal Profile System® which has been developed by Carlson Learning Company of Minneapolis, Minnesota. This Profile presents a plan to help us understand ourselves and others in our social and/or work environment.

This Personal Profile System is a self-administered, self-development instrument. The Profile was originally developed by Dr. John Geier based upon extensive study of our behavioral tendencies and subsequently refined by Dr. Michael O'Connor (Carlson Learning Company, 1993). The Personal Profile also utilizes the work of William Moulton Marston. He had theorized that human behavior could be studied on a two-axis model according to a person's actions in a favorable or an antagonistic environment (Marston, 1979).

The focus of this instrument is to understand oneself so that one can understand others and place oneself in an environment that is conducive to one's success (Kaufman & O'Connor, 1992). This instrument measures four dimensions of behavioral responses (DiSC, Carlson Learning Company, 1994):

- Dominance (D):   emphasis is on shaping the environment by overcoming opposition to accomplish results.

- Influence (i):   emphasis is on shaping the environment by influencing or persuading others.

- Steadiness (S):   emphasis is on cooperation with others to carry out the task.

- Conscientiousness (C):   cautious, tentative response designed to reduce antagonistic factors in an unfavorable environment.

The behavioral dimensions can be divided into two categories — process or product orientation. Persons with predominantly Dominance or Influence tendencies are process oriented. They want to shape the environment according to their particular view. These are individuals who continually test and push the limits set by the group or organization. Those people with the Steadiness and Conscientiousness tendencies are product oriented. They focus on the how and the why. These people may at times need encouragement to reset limits.

For example, people with Dominance tendencies have the results they want well in mind. Their messages are designed to stimulate and prod others to untested action.

They are attentive to communication which will speed up the action. Questions about the "correct" action are shrugged away. These individuals feel they can change the course of action (Performax Systems International, 1986).

People with Influence tendencies also want to shape and mold events and have an active voice. Their messages are designed to stimulate and prod others to action by working with and through people. They are interested in people and like to make people feel good about themselves. They are particularly attentive to the personal needs of others and search for ways in which to meet these needs. Messages about how to actually accomplish a task are often deemed unimportant; these stimuli are at the far range of their attention span.

Persons with Steadiness tendencies are interested in how and when — a product orientation. They send messages which reflect their interest in maintaining a stability within themselves and the situation — between the old and the new. Messages which urge action before knowing how to do things, fall on deaf ears.

Those individuals with the Conscientiousness (to their own standards) tendencies reflect their product orientation when they send messages which ask the reasons for the change. "Why?" is a favorite question. They have concern for doing it "accurately." They are receptive to messages which reassure them they are doing it correctly. Messages which ignore this tend to go unheeded.

How the Personal Profile Contributes to Stress Reduction

The Personal Profile System provides considerable information about the way people respond to stress. This information can be effectively utilized to understand and help reduce stress. As we have seen earlier, in Chapters 1 and 2 the stress response consists of two components: "fight" or "flight." Hans Selye (1956) refined this concept into four distinct responses which correspond to our four primary behavioral tendencies as outlined below:

- Fight - The high "D" will tend to use the fight response. They will attempt to destroy the impact of the stress or eliminate its cause. The fighting may be verbal or physical.

- Flight - The high "i" will tend to use the flight response. They will attempt to flee from the situation. If physical flight is not possible, they will attempt to flee emotionally by changing the subject or ignoring the issue. If the stress continues, they may become emotionally abusive.

- Tolerate - The high "S" will tend to use the tolerate response, which is really a subtle form of flight. They will not attempt to flight or flee, however, they will tend to shut down. They will remain in the situation with apparent calmness, however, they may become dysfunctional, not knowing what to do.

- Avoid - The high "C" will tend to use the avoid response, which is a subtle form of fight. They will not attempt to fight or flee, however, they will tend to withdraw in order to avoid conflict. They may, in fact, use the time as an opportunity to carefully plan their next move.

According to Kaufman and O'Connor (1992), if the level of stress becomes even more severe, the individuals will tend to move step-by-step through the stress responses associated with behavioral styles more directive than their own. That is, a "high i" will first move from the flight response to the tolerate response characteristic of the "high S." This individual will then move from the "tolerate" response to the "avoid" response to the "fight" response characteristic of the "high D." A "high S" individual will move through the "avoid" response to the "fight" response. A "high C" individual will move to the "fight" response. The "fight" response is the ultimate survival-level response. We will all resort to that behavior if the level of stress is high enough.

Note. Information on behavioral styles is adapted from the widely-used DiSC Dimensions of Behavior Model and the Personal Profile System. ® ©Copyright 1994, Carlson Learning Company.

For further information and training on the Personal Profile System, one may contact J.A.R. and Associates, Management, Training, & Health Consultants, 407 West Eighth Street, Suite 333, Mankato, MN, 56001, (507) 345-8822 (Ph.), (507) 345-8534 (Fax).

Stress Management Principle # 4

We need to think first before passing judgement.

Summary Points

- We spend approximately two thirds of our waking hours in communicating.

- Faulty communication is at the root of most stress.

- A popular model of communication described by Berlo is known as SMCR (Sender, Message, Channel, Receiver) Model.

- An important aspect of communication is assertiveness or the ability to say "no" without feeling guilty.

- Being assertive produces the least amount of stress. While being passive or aggressive are more stressful.

- Assertiveness is an acquired quality and all of us can learn to be assertive.

- Some of the techniques for becoming assertive include: sounding like a broken record, compromising, providing free information, self disclosure, fogging, negative assertion, and negative inquiry.

- How we behave impacts upon how effectively we communicate.

- The Personal Profile System is a tool to assess our behavioral styles. The Profile describes four responses: Dominance (D), Influence (i), Steadiness (S), and Conscientiousness (C).

References and Further Readings

Allessandra, T., O'Connor, M.J., & Allessandra, J. (1990). <u>People smart: powerful techniques for turning every encounter into a mutual win.</u> LaJolla, CA: Keynote Publishing Company.

Berlo, D.K. (1960). <u>The process of communication.</u> New York, NY: Holt, Rinehart and Winston.

Bower, S.A., & Bower, G.H. (1976). <u>Asserting yourself</u>. Reading, MA: Addison Wesley Publishing Company.

Burke, C.R., Hall, D.R., & Hawley, D. (1986). <u>Living with stress</u>. Clackamas, OR: Wellsource, Inc.

Carlson Learning Company. (1993). <u>The Personal Profile System</u>. Minneapolis, MN: Carlson Learning Company, Inc.

Davis, M., Eshelman, E.R., McKay, M. (1982). <u>The relaxation and stress reduction workbook</u>. (2nd ed.). Oakland, CA: New Harbinger Publications.

Green, L.W., & Kreuter, M.W. (1991). <u>Health promotion planning. An educational and environmental approach</u>. (2nd ed). Mountain View, CA: Mayfield Publishing Company.

Greenberg, J.S. (1993). <u>Comprehensive Stress management</u>. (4th ed). Dubuque, IA: William C. Brown Publishers.

Kaufman, D. & O'Connor, M.J. (1992). <u>Basic questions and answer guide for needs motivated behavior</u>. Minneapolis, MN: Carlson Marketing Group.

Lazarus, A. (1966). Behavioral rehearsal vs. nondirective therapy vs. advice in effecting behavior change. <u>Behavioral Research and Therapy, 4</u>, 209-212.

Marston, W.M. (1979). <u>Emotions of normal people</u>. Minneapolis, MN: Personal Press, Inc.

Mucchielli, R. (1970). <u>Introduction to structural psychology</u>. New York, NY: Funk & Wagnalls.

Myers, P. & Nance, D. (1991). <u>The upset book</u>. (2nd ed.). Wichita, KS: Mac Press.

O'Connor, M.J. & Merwin, S.J. (1992). <u>The mysteries of motivation: Why people do the things they do</u>. Minneapolis, MN Carlson Learning Company.

References and Further Readings (Cont'd)

Performax Systems International. (1986). The personal profile system manual and behavioral patterns master guide. Minneapolis, MN: Carlson Learning Company.

Rathus, S.A. (1973). A 30 item schedule for assessing assertive behavior. Behavior Therapy, 4, 398-406.

Robbins, S.P. (1991). Organizational behavior: Concepts, controversies, and applications. (5th ed.). Englewood Cliffs, NJ: Prentice Hall.

Rokeach, M. (1970). Beliefs, attitudes and values. San Francisco, CA: Jossey Bass.

Selye, H. (1956). The stress of life. New York, NY: McGraw-Hill Book Company.

Smith, M.J. (1975). When I say no, I feel guilty. New York, NY: Bantam Books.

Wolpe, J. (1958). Psychotherapy by reciprocal inhibition. Stanford, CA: Stanford University Press.

Yogananda, P. (1946). Autobiography of a yogi. Los Angeles, CA: Self-Realization Fellowship.

* * * * * * * * * * * * * *

CHAPTER 5

MANAGING ANGER AND RESOLVING CONFLICTS

A Poison Tree

I was angry with my friend
I told my wrath, my wrath did end.
I was angry with my foe:
I told it not, my wrath did grow.

William Blake

What Is Anger?

Anger is an emotion, which if not managed, neutralized, or controlled, can result in great suffering for oneself, as well as for others. Uncontrolled anger results in release of various hormones and neurotransmitters. As a consequence, blood pressure rises, cardiac muscles contract, and gastric secretions increase. Eventually the by-products produced do not get used in the system and accumulate causing harm to the body. This can manifest itself in the form of various illnesses such as hypertension, peptic ulcer, stroke, and others. Psychologically, uncontrolled anger "poisons the mind" and makes us perform many actions which we may regret later. At the societal level anger is at the root of many wars, terrorist activities, riots, looting, arson, and so on. Therefore, the anger which originates within the mind gradually engulfs the body, the family and eventually has devastating effects on society. However, some anger within limits and with full awareness is beneficial too because it protects the human organism. The key, however, is to have <u>balance</u> with anger. In this chapter we will discuss how to attain this balance.

Most of us tend to "blow up" at the slightest provocation. Later we regret our behavior when it is usually too late. According to Smith (1993), when considering anger, it is useful to begin by making some distinctions. Anger which results in aggression is destructive <u>behavior</u>. However, anger is essentially an internal <u>feeling</u>. While it is often appropriate to monitor and control aggressive behavior, feelings cannot always be controlled. It is important to realize that the feeling of anger can serve as a useful warning sign that we may be about to engage in aggressive or self-destructive behavior. Therefore, it is important to manage one's anger and attain a state of balance.

We have a number of diagnostic tests available for various medical disorders, but unfortunately no standard test is available for diagnosing anger. Moreover, a number of questions about anger continue to perplex and challenge us. For example, do we consider whether or not angry people are sick? Does getting angry make us feel better? If we let our anger out, what are the consequences? If we hold our anger in, what are the consequences?

Managing the Anger Within

Most psychologists agree that if we become angry, we must feel that anger. There is no point in denying, hiding, repressing, or suppressing that anger. This overt feeling is a natural process. We can appreciate that a newborn infant expresses these emotions of anger and rage by crying right at the time of birth. Throughout all ages or periods of development, many humans confront almost daily their own feelings of anger and those of other people with whom they come in contact. It is generally accepted today that we need our anger to protect us from a hostile and aggressive world.

Unfortunately, what we generally tend to do while dealing with anger within is: (1) Feel the anger, but sit on it, deny it, and repress it; or (2) Feel the anger and freely express it. Denial and repression of our anger does not get us anywhere and "uncontrolled rage" leads to far more harm.

A well-known model to manage anger is based upon the concepts of Rational Emotive Therapy (R.E.T.) developed by Albert Ellis (1975, 1977). He proposed the hydraulic theory, which states that anger and other emotions have a tendency to increase in intensity, to expand under pressure like steam in a kettle, so that if we "squelch" our emotions, if we do not give free vent to them, we run the risk of doing some real harm to ourselves. Real physical harm such as stomach ulcers, high blood pressure, or other ailments, including severe psychosomatic reactions, may ensue.

Conversely, if we let ourselves feel authentically angry (free expression) and let others know about our feelings, we may frequently encounter problems of quite another nature. People will receive our free expression of anger in most instances as an outwardly aggressive or hostile action, and will probably close themselves off from us and defensively respond to us with further hostility. Some therapists in the field have attempted to solve the problem with still another alternative, what they call creative aggression (or constructive anger). This differs from the above free expression method in that we express ourselves in a controlled and dignified manner and hope that others will willingly listen to our point of view.

Therefore, we can appreciate, that holding in our anger, and not expressing it, is not a worthwhile idea. Free expression of anger also creates a whole complex of other counterproductive problems. Further, we have noted that creative aggression seems a more workable solution but that it still shares some of the same problems. According to Ellis (1977) another alternative, that of "Christian forgiveness," involves the turning of the other cheek. But in this aggressive, often hostile world in which we live, this seems somewhat impractical.

According to Albert Ellis (1977) anger begets anger. Therefore, the most practical solution in dealing with our anger within is that we need to become annoyed and irritated, so that we can become more effective at solving problems. We get angry, then we try to fix the problem. Then we get upset with our own anger, and now we develop a problem with the anger and its consequences. When we become angry, we either "let it out," or "hold it in." A third choice is to become annoyed and irritated, thus we can solve problems. Ellis and Harper (1975) suggests that many people create irrational beliefs about what we should and should not do regarding anger. Research shows that when some people become angry, they need to reach closure immediately. For others, it is necessary to be alone, take time out, and work out the anger for themselves. Actually, in our culture we do not seem to have the best vocabulary to define those intense feelings we identify as anger. When people become angry, they often say, "you did that," rather than "I get annoyed" when you do that. Anger comes from a belief that the world should not be the way it is and should be the way I want it to be. This really means to acknowledge the fact that all people have the freedom of will to choose to behave badly. If people do not have free will, then moral philosophy need not exist. When people behave badly, they have that right. No matter how many laws exist, one can never take away a person's free will. Ellis's school of thought suggests to acknowledge and accept what others are by seeing these differences and becoming annoyed and irritated with these differences (Dryden & DiGiuseppe, 1990; Walen, DiGiuseppe, & Wessler, 1980). This <u>annoyance and irritation</u> on our part is often helpful in managing anger for it helps us attain a balance with anger.

Thoughts for Reflection 5.2

What Anger Is. . .

- An emotional response

Anger is an emotional reaction which normally happens in response to an unfulfilled desire, an unmet expectation, and an unimagined consequence.

- A warning signal

Anger helps us to identify that something is wrong and is preventing us from achieving our goals.

- A way to new learning

Usually anger facilitates our power of reflection and opens a door to new learning, provided that we have an open mind and are willing to learn.

- A normal feeling

Anger is a normal response which all of us experience and it is not abnormal to be angry.

- Healthy within limits

Since anger is a feeling, if it is contained and not let out as a behavior, then it serves to release pent up emotions. However, we need not deny, repress, or suppress anger for it to be healthy.

- A protective mechanism

Anger helps all living beings to protect themselves from unconducive surroundings and situations.

- Useful within limits

Anger helps us in setting interactive boundaries with people around us. It serves an important purpose in letting others appreciate what we like and what we dislike.

* * * * * * * * * * * * * *

Thoughts for Reflection 5.2

What Anger Is Not. . .

- Not a problem solving tool

  When we are angry, we should not attempt to solve problems because anger does not help us in arriving at solutions. In fact, anger colors our perception and we deviate from appropriate solutions.

- Not an outlet for revenge

  If anger is suppressed, it tends to make one vengeful and this is not an appropriate response. It causes more harm than good.

- Not projection

  We should not blame others for our anger because anger is basically an internal feeling which originates within our mind and has little to do with the outside world.

- Not being violent

  Anger is not an excuse for being violent. One should exercise adequate control on oneself and one's anger in not being violent especially with innocent people, children, and so on.

- Not a way of control

  By being angry we cannot control anyone else. We may, in the short run, create a sense of temporary fear which may look like us having control, but in the long run it never works.

- Not healthy if exceeds limits

  Anger has been associated with a number of medical disorders, especially if it is uncontrolled.

- Not useful if inappropriate

  Anger is counterproductive. Anger loses its utility if one gets angry too frequently or without proper reason.

* * * * * * * * * * * * * * *

Anger and Stress: The Connection

As we have identified in Chapter 1 the stress response has <u>two</u> <u>components</u>: "fight" and "flight." The "fight" component of the stress response is a naturally occurring event, which is also responsible for angry behavior. Signs of anger and stress are interchangeable. Both anger and stress lead to anxiety, sleeplessness, uncontrolled thinking, brooding, restlessness, irritability, and so on. Along with these manifestations come headaches, muscle tension, peptic ulcers, and other stress-related problems. More dangerous are the reactions which we cannot feel (Eliot & Breo, 1989).

Another important dimension in the context of anger and stress is our Personality. In Type A personality people, it appears that hostility and anger may be the key (Friedman & Rosenman, 1959, 1974). We have already seen, as shown in Chapter 1, that Type A personality people experience greater stress and the negative sequelae associated with stress. Coronary heart disease and essential hypertension are two important diseases in particular which have been linked with anger. By constantly suppressing their anger, some psychologists believe hypertensives keep their blood pressure elevated. According to Tavris (1982), "release the anger and blood pressure should fall."

Anger also involves the feeling of pain and/or injury to oneself. If we personalize anger, we become fearful, anxious, feel cornered, become further angered, and lose control. This "loss of control" causes us to form judgements, make assumptions, and further escalates our feeling of anger. In order to maintain balance and prevent anger from escalating, we need to preserve our self-worth, keep things in perspective, not unduly feed our fears, and <u>decide</u> to be in control of ourselves. Thus we reserve judgement and are able to maintain a problem-solving attitude. Anger is useful as a <u>signal</u> in which a "warning light" causes us to take action. As a solution, anger rarely helps, for it adds fuel to the fire, heats up the problem, and may cause inappropriate action.

<u>Expectations</u> control our reactions to anger. What we usually expect and which does not happen acts as a "triggering event" and causes a reaction to which we seek a solution. The first time an expectation is not met, we have no idea how to approach this situation, so we think about what to do. If our solution seems to work we try it out again in future situations. Once we are sure our solution works, we no longer wonder about whether it will work and so we stop thinking about it and just do it. In this way, a habit is formed. If we have learned to respond by getting angry, then we will respond in that way irrespective of what the consequences will be. As time passes, reflection on the consequences decreases further and further. We also remind ourselves less and less about what it is that we are to do. This is an efficient way to operate provided that our solution is really a good solution. In the case of anger, it is not a good solution. What really happens is that it causes a "fire" and we have to face the harmful consequences. This response needs to be changed. The following <u>steps</u> are to be considered in effecting this change:

1. Recognize and admit our old solution is not working.

2. Use the old reaction as a cue to start a new search for a new solution.

3. Activate our thinking to identify the expectations upon which we are basing our

reactions, and begin to examine them critically.

4. Examine the validity of our expectations, reject those we find are not true or helpful, and replace them with ones which are.

5. With new expectations the response will change.

6. Keep reinforcing these new expectations over and over again.

In order to manage the anger within, we need to identify situations in which we are likely to be angry. Then we have to look for the <u>cues</u> for anger that trigger an event. Unfulfilled and unrealistic expectations are often at the root of most anger. An understanding of these is helpful in reducing anger. Next we have to analyze the <u>costs</u> and <u>benefits</u> that come after our anger has subsided and the event is over. Managing anger basically involves modifying these cues and consequences, and finding effective replacements for the anger.

Therefore, the first step in managing anger is to find out where we are with anger in our personal lives. Worksheet 5.1 has been designed to help us in enhancing this understanding and Worksheet 5.2 helps us in managing anger.

Thoughts for Reflection 5.3

Points to Ponder

- The troubles of our proud and angry dust
  Are from eternity, and shall not fail.
  Bear them we can, and if we can we must.
  Shoulder the sky, my lad, and drink your ale.

  A.E. Housman

- Anger is never without an argument, but seldom with a good.

  George Savile, Marquis of Halifax

- Anger is one of the sinews of the soul.

  Thomas Fuller

- Where it concerns himself, Who's angry at a slander makes it true.

  Ben Jonson

- He that is slow to anger is better than the mighty; and he that ruleth his
  spirit is he that taketh a city.

  Bible Proverb 32

- Anger makes dull men witty, but it keeps them poor.

  Queen Elizabeth I

Worksheet 5.1
Self Assessment of Anger

Let us respond to the following questions honestly. Responses will serve as a means of feedback for our own improvement to manage anger.

1. Is anger a problem for me?   ___ Yes ___ No ___ Not sure

2. How do I know when I am angry?

_____

_____

_____

_____

_____

3. How do I feel inside when I am angry?

_____

_____

_____

_____

_____

4. What do I do about my anger?

_____

_____

_____

_____

_____

Worksheet 5.1 Self Assessment of Anger (Cont'd)

5. Let me describe the last time when I got angry. At what or with
    whom was I angry? How did this affect me?

_____

_____

_____

_____

_____

6. Let me analyze my reasons for becoming angry?

_____

_____

_____

_____

7. Let me indicate any problems created by my anger.

_____

_____

_____

_____

_____

Worksheet 5.1 Self Assessment of Anger (Cont'd)

8. Let me list other ways I could have solved the problem without getting angry.

_____

_____

_____

_____

_____

_____

* * * * * * * * * * * * * * *

FEEDBACK ON WORKSHEET 5.1

Worksheet 5.1 helps us to acquire a greater insight into the situations and persons with whom we become angry.   If we can identify these situations which cause our anger and the various negative consequences which we have to face as a result of our anger, we become more motivated to change our behavior. This enhanced awareness is the basis and the first step of changing our response to anger.

* * * * * * * * * * * * * *

Worksheet 5.2
Managing Our Anger

The following worksheet has been designed to help us deal with our anger in a more productive way. Let us seek out a quiet place and reflect upon and respond to the following statements.

1. Let us identify a situation in which we have expressed anger inappropriately. Let us analyze our goals and/or desired expectations. We need to then break the situation down into steps. Let us examine at which step the anger became apparent.

Situation:

_____

_____

_____

_____

Goals/Desired Expectations:

_____

_____

Steps in the Event:

_____

_____

_____

_____

2. Let us describe the benefits which this anger had.

_____

_____

Worksheet 5.2 Dealing with Our Anger (Cont'd)

3.   Did the anger cost us anything or cause any harm?

_____

_____

_____

4.   Do the costs outweigh the benefits? _____ Yes _____ No

5.   What alternative step(s) could we have taken instead of the one in which we got angry and still met our goal/desired expectation?

_____

_____

6.   What were the barriers which prevented us from adopting this alternative step?

_____

_____

_____

_____

7.   How can we overcome these barriers in the future?

_____

_____

_____

_____

* * * * * * * * * * * * * *

Dealing with an Angry Person

1. Transactional Analysis

Eric Berne (1967) described a technique called Transactional Analysis (T.A.) which is a method for understanding interpersonal transactions. Transactions are defined as units of social intercourse.

An understanding of the basics of this method will enhance our skills to deal with anger within ourself, as well as, relate better with an angry person. According to Transactional Analysis, the various aspects of our personalities can be classified into three states:

(a) The Child Ego State. This is the state in which we enter the world. Within the child state are three dimensions: (1) The free child which is inquisitive, wants to have fun, be liked, and be admired; (2) The rebellious child which has been acquired because of certain experiences in our childhood and rebels against domination; and (3) The manipulative child which has developed as a result of our learning some manipulative behavior in order to get our needs fulfilled as children. An angry person is almost always in the child ego state — rebellious or manipulative, and this ego state needs to be addressed first.

(b) The Parent Ego State. This is the repository for the events as we perceived them in the early years of our lives, up to five years of age. These recordings or parent tapes owe their origin to our parents and other significant people during our childhood who told us what to do and what not to do. These messages are resolved without editing and include all prohibitions, admonitions, and rules set by example or stated. The parent ego state has two parts: (1) The critical parent which results in pronouncement of most imperatives like, "you should," "you must," "you ought to," etc., and (2) The nurturing or caring parent which sympathizes, listens, encourages and exhibits care and love.

(c) The Adult Ego State. This is not synonymous with maturity. However, this is the rational part of us and operates on data gathering and analysis. It is unemotional and helps us look at things through facts and objectivity.

The most interesting aspect of this theory is that all of us possess these stages within ourselves. What happens with anger is that we transcend into the child ego state. However, sometimes we may not appear childlike because we have camouflaged our feelings as either "critical parents," "caring parents," or "rational adults." If masquerading as a "critical parent," we tend to use what we should have done or ought to be doing. In the mask of "caring parent" we tend to be sarcastic. In the mask of a "rational adult" ego state, we may try to give justification and rationalization which may actually be biased, and underneath might be a burning inferno. Besides, other emotions like worry and fear, bereavement may also appear like anger, but needs to be addressed in a different way.

With this understanding it is clear that in anger a person is in a "child" ego state and this should be addressed first. It can be tackled by a "caring parent" response followed by a "rational adult" response. The problem occurs when we respond as a "critical parent" or evoke our "child" ego state or move directly to the adult stage bypassing the "caring parent." These responses do not extinguish anger but only flair it up further. Evoking a "caring parent" response helps the angry person to be at ease and feel that their behavior has been addressed. When this is followed by a "rational adult" response, then an understanding by the angry person of his or her "mistake(s)" occurs. In this way this approach helps to disarm any angry person.

For example, a fellow student or fellow worker becomes angry with us on some event and stops speaking. If we do not speak to that person it is likely to add to the existing anger. However, if we approach that person with a caring attitude and inquiries about the reason for his or her anger, it is likely that he or she will narrate the event from his or her perspective. Having re-established this rapport and understood the problem from the other person's perspective we can <u>rationally</u> analyze the situation and thus resolve the anger between both of us.

2. The "Time Out" Procedure

Often, when we are angry, we do not think. In order to reactivate our thinking, we need to put aside everything in which we are engaged and find time to reflect and introspect. The "Time Out" Procedure detailed below (Veenstra & Coursol, 1986) provides us with this opportunity to reflect upon our actions, then accordingly, change them. It consists of the following steps:

(a) <u>Stop</u>: We have to immediately put a stop to our conventional behavior. This implies that we can no longer respond by getting angry at situations in which we got angry earlier. This determination to "stop" is the first step in the "Time Out" Procedure.

(b) <u>Think</u>: Having stopped our conventional response, we need to think about a new approach in dealing with situations which may potentiate anger. Think about this new way by identifying and describing the new skills which will be required. Also think about the approaches and possible barriers in acquiring these new skills.

(c) <u>Act</u>: Overcome the cognitive barriers (i.e. faulty beliefs and expectations) which stand in our way to implement the new way. Having overcome the barriers, act on the new way by practising the new skills.

The effectiveness of the "Time Out" Procedure is based upon the other person's view of the position which we have taken. A person's perception is a factor here in that once we attempt to practice the "Time Out" Procedure, it is up to the other person to react to us. An angry person wants to get his or her point across to us. This provides that person with a relief from their sense of injustice. This also gives hope that the problem-solving process has started. What an angry person usually gets is a counterattack explaining why he or she was wrong. Since the "defense of self" is a priority, an angry person does not listen (Veenstra & Coursol, 1986). What an angry person does in response is defend self and attack more intensely. His or her anger is increased because of the pain felt of not getting through. The angry person becomes apprehensive that the problem will continue unsolved. In the "Time Out" Procedure (Veenstra & Coursol, 1986) options which are helpful when listening to an angry person consist of the following:

- <u>Reflective or Empathic Listening</u>. "What you are saying is . . ." In this approach we are serving like a mirror, acknowledging what the other person is saying but not putting out our own view as a target. Our own viewpoint is preserved and set aside from consideration.

- <u>Possible Agreement or Fogging</u>. "Let me think about that . . ." In this approach we acknowledge that the other person might be on target but we are not committing ourselves definitely. It is important to follow through on problem solving so the other person will not see it as a stall.

- <u>Actual Agreement or Admitting That We Are Wrong</u>. "You are right, it was wrong for me to . . . " In this approach you acknowledge that the other person is on target and admit that we are wrong and at fault. If we don't really believe we are wrong, this will only "stuff" and not solve the problem.

- <u>Negative Inquiry or Inviting Further Criticism</u>. "Are there other things I do that hurt you . . .?" In this approach we give an opportunity to have the other person aim at the target. This must be done genuinely.

This valuable technique which has been shown to effectively manage anger is the "Time Out" Procedure as shown in Figure 5-1.

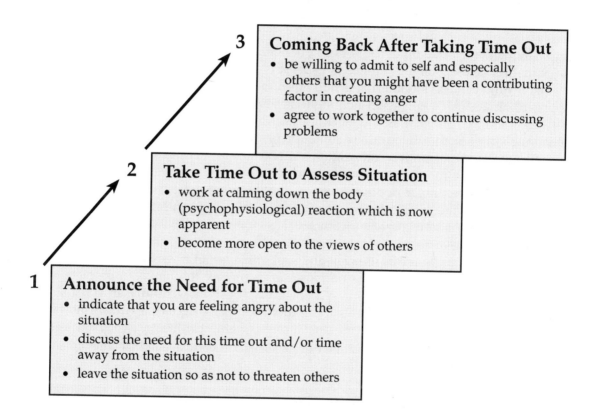

Figure 5-1 The "Time Out" Procedure

3. The "Upset" Philosophy

According to Myers and Nance (1991) angry people are usually "upset." Moreover, we also become "upset" when we have to deal with an angry person. We can cope with an angry person if we can identify and understand the specific incident that triggered their anger. We will also have success in preventing another person from becoming angry if we understand the kinds of situations that are likely to be anger provoking.

Anger is the result of many factors, including the triggering or precipitating situation, our past experiences, individual responses to experiences, and idiosyncrasies. Understanding what creates anger in another person is often helpful both in planning preventive strategies and in deciding how to handle anger once it occurs. Therefore, we have to examine the situation of the other person. We have to step into the shoes of the other person and then look at the situation from his or her angle.

Myers and Nance (1991) have identified several triggering factors and events. They are:

1. Dependency. Usually a feeling of dependence on another person, object, or thing can lead to increased anger. Anger is especially accentuated when we are intimately dependent and cannot find alternatives to our dependency. Such a person can be helped by providing enough choices and helping that person to become more independent.

2. Authority. Authority normally comes by position, expertise, or wealth. Oftentimes authority makes a person inappropriately authoritarian. People who are authoritarian tend to utilize their authority in a manner which provokes anger. It is the way they say things which creates anger in others. It may not be what they say but how they say it which precipitates anger. Therefore, one needs to be very careful in how one is presenting a point of view and using one's authority.

3. Unclear Limits. Some of us want and seek direction in how we perform our tasks. These directions can come from our parents, our peers, our teachers, our employers, our colleagues, our spouses, and so on. When these directions are unclear, confusing, or dualistic, then it leads to anger and frustration. Anger originating from this type of unclarity can be dealt with by setting specific directions and limits. If these directions come from within ourselves, then greater autonomy and control can be achieved in dealing with anger.

4. Complexity. Many situations are apparently complicated, intricate, and complex. If we get stuck in the complexity, then we are prone to get angry. This type of anger can be tackled, simplifying the process by breaking it down into smaller parts or steps. Breaking down any complicated event into smaller parts or steps often simplifies the process. We need to constantly remember that life is essentially a simple process.

5. Prior Unresolved Conflict. Past events are an important source of our anger, especially events on which we have not reached closure or which have not been resolved amicably. These events and associated anger keeps surfacing again and again. Until and unless these conflicts are completely resolved, sublimation of anger cannot result. We need to put our mind and effort toward resolving conflicts which we can. We need to strengthen our mind to "forgive" and "forget" the conflicts over which we have no control.

6. <u>Communication Problems</u>. We have seen in Chapter 4 that poor, ineffective, and marginal communication often leads to stress and anger. If we are not able to communicate effectively, it causes anger and frustration in us as well as others. This poor communication can result from a number of causes. Some of these causes may pertain to us while others may pertain to others. While we cannot do much about how others communicate, we can certainly improve upon our own communication, especially, when this miscommunication is an intended one, for some inexplicable reasons on our part. As far as possible we should try to identify these reasons, overcome them, and make our communication as clear and effective as possible.

7. <u>Conflict of Interest</u>. People have different ideas and interests. Sometimes when a task needs to be achieved, these differences tend to be mutually conflicting. This conflict can be a source of anger and frustration. Therefore, all potential conflicts need to be resolved. Thoughts for Reflection 5.4 and 5.5 provide us with some suggestions for resolving conflicts.

Thoughts for Reflection 5.4

Five Conflict-Handling Orientations

Conflict Handling Orientation	Appropriate Situations
1. Competition	• When quick, decisive action is vital • On the important issues where unpopular actions need implementing • On issues vital to the organization's welfare and when you know you're right • Against people who take advantage of non competitive behavior
2. Collaboration	• To find an integrative solution when both sets of concerns are too important to be compromised • When your objective is to learn • To merge insights from people with different perspectives • To gain commitment by incorporating concerns into a consensus • To work through feelings that have interfered with a relationship
3. Avoidance	• When an issue is trivial, or more important issues are pressing • When you perceive no chance of satisfying your concerns • When potential disruption outweighs the benefits of resolution • To let people cool down and regain perspective • When gathering information supersedes immediate decision • When others can resolve the conflict more effectively • When issues seem tangential or symptomatic of other issues
4. Accommodate	• When you find you are wrong to allow better position to be heard, to learn, and to show your reasonableness • When issues are more important to others than yourself to satisfy others and maintain cooperation • To build social credits for later issues • To minimize loss when you are outmatched and losing • When harmony and stability are especially important • To allow subordinates to develop by learning from mistakes

Thoughts for Reflection 5.4

Five Conflict-Handling Orientations (Cont'd)

5. Compromise
- When goals are important but not worth the effort or potential disruption of more assertive modes
- When opponents with equal power are committed to mutually exclusive goals
- To achieve temporary settlements to complex issues
- To arrive at expedient solutions under time pressure
- As a backup when collaboration or competition is unsuccessful

Note. From "Toward multidimensional values in teaching: The example of conflict behaviors" by K.W. Thomas, July 1977, Academy of Management Review, p.487. Copyright 1977 by Academy of Management Review. Reprinted by permission.

Thoughts for Reflection 5.5

Resolving Conflicts by Managing Anger

Once we have some idea of what anger is and what causes it, we are ready to think about a process for defusing anger in other people. Some of these methods for dealing with anger include:

- <u>Listening</u>. We really have to work at listening. Listen for the content, the feelings, and those things with which you can agree. Listen without your critical parent, without personalizing, and without counterattacking. Cover your hot buttons, and cover your rear.

- <u>Acknowledge Feelings</u>. Acknowledge that the other person is angry. Do not try to talk him or her out of feeling angry. Simply understand what the person is experiencing.

- <u>Agreeing</u>. State areas of agreement. This involves a different mindset. It means that we are not listening to catch the other person when they exaggerate, get confused, or overreact. Rather, we are listening for those things with which we can agree.

- <u>Getting Agreement on the Problem</u>. It is important to get some agreement on the problem.

- <u>Finding Solutions</u>. Agreeing first on the problem, identifying possible solutions, and then agreeing on one solution.

- <u>Closing</u>. "Is there anything else I can do?" "Are you feeling satisfied at the outcome?" "Let me know what else I can do." Thank the person for letting you know that they were angry. It helps to keep things straight between us. When you know what the problem is, a better chance of solving it exists.

<u>Note</u>. From <u>The upset book</u> (2nd ed.), (p. 103-131), by P. Myers and D. Nance., 1991. Wichita, KS. Mac Press. Copyright 1991 by Pennie Myers and Don Nance. Adapted by permission.

* * * * * * * * * * * * * * *

4. Active Listening

An important factor in managing anger is the ability to listen actively. Active listening is an intervention which addresses our interaction with others (Steinmetz, Blankenship, Brown, Hall, & Miller, 1980). This is an effective yet simple tool for managing anger and thereby reducing stress. Its applicability has multifarious uses.

First, active listening is a <u>diagnostic tool</u>. It helps one to identify and pinpoint the cause or reason for the other person's anger. Second, active listening is a <u>disarming device</u> which helps the angry person to appropriately "let out" his or her feelings. Third, active listening provides an opportunity to seek <u>clarification</u> which is an important component for resolving anger. Fourth, active listening aids to <u>rationalize</u>, develop <u>clear thinking</u>, and <u>communicate effectively</u> in order to mutually resolve anger. Finally, active listening helps the angry person to preserve his or her <u>dignity</u> and not express anger in an undignified manner.

Worksheet 5.3 has been designed to help us deal more effectively with an angry person through active listening. Since this worksheet involves role-playing, it cannot be completed alone and requires the cooperation of a partner.

Worksheet 5.3
Learning Active Listening

In order to practice active listening, we will require the cooperation of a partner. This activity involves role-playing and sharpening our skills to listen actively. Let us ask our partner to imagine a situation in which he or she was or will be angry with us. Let him or her imagine that situation mentally. We, as well as our partner, will have to work at this role-play. Following are some of the guidelines for us to work on.

<u>Self</u>	<u>Partner</u>
• <u>Direct questioning:</u> Start probing the reasons for the partner's anger in a calm and controlled manner.	• Since you are angry, you may choose to respond or not respond.
• <u>Rationalizing</u>: Try to understand the partner's feelings. Also try to understand the reasons and explanations for this behavior in our own mind.	• Act out the way you actually feel.
• <u>Clarifying</u>: We may want to seek clarification on our partner's feelings and responses.	• Behave the way you feel.
• <u>Supporting</u>: As far as possible let us try to support our partner's viewpoint. This may be difficult, but let us attempt to do it.	• You may choose whether or not to yield to the responses.

FEEDBACK ON WORKSHEET 5.3

Both of us need to focus on the way we are feeling now. Has the anger been resolved? If yes, discuss the reasons. If no, discuss why not? We may want to document in the space below some of our learnings from this experience.

_____

_____

_____

_____

_____

_____

_____

_____

_____

_____

_____

_____

_____

We may want to reinforce these learnings from time to time so that they become a part of our behavior, and then we can deal with an angry person more effectively. Our partner may want to change roles with us and improve his or her ability at dealing with angry people.

* * * * * * * * * * * * * *

Thoughts for Reflection 5.6

Calming Reminders

1. Let us not take anger personally. Let us maintain a sense of self-worth. Let us ask ourselves:

    - "Are they having a rough day?"
    - "Is this really directed to me?"
    - "They are just criticizing my behavior, not my being."

2. Let us keep anger in perspective. Let us not feed our fears. Let us tell ourselves:

    - "Relax, you can make it through this."
    - "It is not going to be the end of the world."
    - "It is not that bad."

3. Let us decide to be in control of ourselves. Let us repeat to ourselves:

    - "I shall not let the anger control me."
    - "I can and will control the anger."

4. Let us not be judgmental. Let us ask ourselves:

    - "Do I need to attribute reasons?"
    - "Am I expecting too much in this situation?"
    - "Can anyone always win?"

5. Let us maintain a problem-solving attitude. Let us ask ourselves:

    - "Do I have an open mind?"
    - "What are the alternatives?"

* * * * * * * * * * * * * * *

Thoughts for Reflection 5.7

The Value of "I" Messages

If we start a statement with an "I," it implies we are owning responsibility. If we start a statement with "you," that implies that we are shifting responsibility to the other person. Every "you" message can be turned into an "I" message. Then it becomes a nonblaming statement about one's own self. Of course, one cannot always talk in calm "I" messages all the time. There is no distinct advantage in using "I" messages for all situations. If our goal is to let the other person know that we are angry, we can do it in our own personal style, and our style may do the job. If, however, our goal is to break a pattern in an important relationship and/or to develop a stronger sense of self that we can bring to all our relationships, it is essential that we learn to translate our anger into clear, nonblaming statements about our own self, that is, "I" statements (Lerner, 1985).

* * * * * * * * * * * * * *

Stress Management Principle # 5

Balancing our anger balances our life.

Summary Points

- Unmanaged anger is harmful to self and others.

- Anger is an internal <u>feeling</u> which, if not managed, results in aggression which is a destructive <u>behavior</u>.

- Denying, repressing, or even freely expressing anger are often harmful.

- In order to manage anger within ourselves, through Rational Emotive Therapy as described by Albert Ellis, we need to become <u>annoyed</u> and <u>irritated</u>. This annoyance and irritation helps us to attain balance with anger.

- Unfulfilled and unrealistic expectations are at the root of anger. An understanding of these often leads to decreased anger.

- Transactional Analysis, first described by Eric Berne, is a useful technique in dealing with an angry person.

- According to Transactional Analysis, our personalities have three ego states: "child" (free, rebellious, manipulative), "parent" (critical, caring), and "adult" (rational).

- A "caring parent" response followed by a "rational adult," is often helpful in extinguishing the anger of an angry person.

- The "Time Out" Procedure, or giving oneself adequate time to reflect and introspect on dealing with an angry person, is often a helpful approach.

- The "Upset" philosophy, described by Myers and Nance, recognizes several triggering factors for anger: dependency, authority, unclear limits, complexity, prior unresolved conflict, communication problems, and conflict of interest.

- Five conflict handling orientations are: competition, collaboration, avoidance, accommodation, and compromise.

- Active listening is an effective tool to disarm any angry person. It involves direct questioning, rationalizing, clarifying, and supporting.

References and Further Readings

Davis, M., Eshelman, E.R., & McKay, M. (1982). <u>The relaxation and stress reduction workbook</u>. (2nd ed.). Oakland, CA: New Harbinger Publications.

Dryden, W. & DiGiuseppe, R. (1990). <u>A primer on rational-emotive therapy</u>. Champaign, IL: Research Press.

Eliot, R.S., & Breo, D.L. (1989). <u>Is it worth dying for? How to make stress work for you - not against you</u>. New York, NY: Bantam Books.

Ellis, A. (1975). <u>How to live with a neurotic</u>. North Hollywood, CA: Wilshire Book Company.

Ellis, A. (1977). <u>Anger: How to live with and without it</u>. Secaucus, NJ: Citadel Press.

Ellis, A., & Harper, R.A. (1975). <u>A new guide to rational living</u>. North Hollywood, CA: Wilshire Book Company.

Friedman, M., & Rosenman, R.H. (1959). Association of specific overt behavior pattern with blood and cardiovascular findings: Blood clotting time, incidence of arcus senilis & clinical coronary artery disease. <u>Journal of American Medical Association, 169</u>, 1286-1296.

Friedman, M., & Rosenman, R.H. (1974). <u>Type A behavior and your heart</u>. New York, NY: Fawcett Crest.

Greenberg, J.S. (1993). <u>Comprehensive stress management</u>. (3rd. ed.). Dubuque, IA: Wm. C. Brown Publishers.

Lerner, H.G. (1985). <u>The dance of anger</u>. New York, NY: Harper & Row Publishers.

Myers, P., & Nance, D. (1991). <u>The upset book</u>. (2nd ed.). Wichita, KS: Mac Press.

Smith, J.C. (1993). <u>Creative stress management: The 1-2-3 cope system</u>. Englewood Cliffs, NJ: Prentice-Hall, Inc.

Steinmetz, J. Blankenship, J., Brown,L., Hall, D., & Miller, G. (1980). <u>Managing stress before it manages you</u>. Palo Alto, CA: Bull Publishing Company.

Tavris, C. (1982). <u>Anger: The misunderstood emotion</u>. New York, NY: Simon & Schuster, Inc.

Veenstra, G.J. & Coursol, D.H. (1986, August). Cognitive techniques in marital therapy: applications to anger control. Paper presented at The American Psychological Association Convention, Washington, D.C.

Veenstra, G.J. & Coursol, D.H. (1987, August). Levels of therapist involvement with angry couples. Paper presented at The American Psychological Convention, New York, N.Y.

Walen, S.R., DiGiuseppe, R., & Wessler, R.L. (1980). <u>A practitioner's guide to rational-emotive therapy</u>. New York, NY: Oxford University Press.

CHAPTER 6

COPING WITH ANXIETY

To John Dryden of Chesterton

How blessed is he, who leads a country life,
Unvex'd with anxious cares, and void of strife!
Who studying peace, and shunning civil rage,
Enjoy'd his youth, and now enjoys his age:
All who deserve his love, he makes his own;
And, to be lov'd himself, needs only to be known.

John Dryden

What Is Anxiety?

Anxiety is an inevitable part of life. Inherent in anxiety are two components — inefficiency and fear. <u>Inefficiency</u> is the loss of one's mental alertness and inability to gear the mind toward problem solving. <u>Fear</u> is to imagine the consequences of one's own actions always resulting in bad or painful consequences, or to imagine only possible adverse events (Maharishi, 1989). Greenberg (1993) has described anxiety, operationally, as an unrealistic fear resulting in physiological arousal and accompanied by the behavioral signs of escape or avoidance. When this feeling of anxiety gets uncontrolled or excessive, then it knocks one down. Various mental disorders are associated with excessive anxiety. Generalized Anxiety Disorder is characterized by unrealistic or excessive anxiety and worry about life situations. Some of the symptoms of this disorder are (Diagnostic and statistical manual of mental disorders - DSM IV, 1994):

1. Trembling, twitching, feeling shaky
2. Muscle tension, aches, soreness
3. Restlessness
4. Easy fatiguability
5. Shortness of breath
6. Palpitations, feeling of heart beating faster
7. Sweating
8. Dryness of mouth
9. Dizziness, light headedness
10. Nausea
11. Flushes
12. Frequent urination
13. Trouble in swallowing, "lump in throat"
14. Feeling "keyed up" or "on edge"
15. Difficulty concentrating
16. Irritability
17. Trouble falling or staying asleep

In some rural areas and subpopulations of this country, patients use unique descriptions to describe anxiety like "I got the churnings," "I'm uptight," or "I am always freaking out" (Shader & Greenblatt, 1993).

Another type of anxiety disorder is panic disorder. The key symptoms associated with panic attacks are (DSM IV, 1994):

1. Shortness of breath, smothering sensation
2. Dizziness, unsteady feelings, or faintness
3. Palpitations
4. Trembling, shaking
5. Sweating
6. Choking
7. Nausea, abdominal distress
8. Depersonalization, Derealization
9. Numbness, tingling sensations
10. Flushes
11. Chest pain
12. Fear of dying
13. Fear of going crazy or doing something uncontrolled

Panic disorders may occur alone or in conjunction with a secondary syndrome termed "agoraphobia" which is defined as a fear of being in places or situations from which escape might be difficult or embarrassing or in which help might not be available in the event of a panic attack. Affected persons usually restrict their travel or need a companion when they are away from home or other familiar places. The severity of avoidance behavior can range from mild, where there is distress, to severe, where the person is completely homebound.

Population-based surveys about emotional disorders in the United States have revealed a one-year period prevalence of anxiety among adults between 5 to 15 percent and panic disorders between 1 to 2 percent (Regier et al., 1988).

These are, however, representations of pathological conditions which require treatment with benzodiazepines and other drugs. In this chapter we will learn about the mechanisms to prevent these conditions from occurring. It requires a systematic and regular practice in order to cope with worrying and anxiety so that these feelings do not get out of proportion and result in disorders. By one's learning these practical techniques, worrying and anxiety can be reduced and long lasting health and happiness can be maintained in life.

Before we proceed to learn these techniques, let us take the Taylor Manifest Anxiety Scale in Worksheet 6.1 which measures the degree to which we manifest anxiety.

Thoughts for Reflection 6.1

When You Worry Think!

- Why do you worry unnecessarily? Who is it that you fear? Who can kill you? The soul is immortal.

- Whatever has happened has been good. Whatever is happening is good. Whatever will happen will be good. Do not regret the past. Do not worry about the future.

- What is it that you have lost? What did you bring that you have lost? What did you create that is now no more? You did not bring anything to this world. Whatever you took you took here. You came empty-handed and you will go empty-handed. Whatever belongs to you today belonged to someone else yesterday and will belong to someone else tomorrow. The cause of your misery is the illusory happiness which you derive by thinking about the things which you own.

- Change is a rule of nature. What you think is death, is actually life. Remove mine and yours, small and big from your mind. Then everything is yours, and you are for everyone.

- This body does not belong to you and neither do you belong to this body. This body is made of elements found in nature and will go back into nature.

- Whatever you do, do it with a sense of detachment without owning and then you will always feel free and happy.

Note. Adapted from Eastern philosophy from India as described in Bhagvad Gita, The Holy Scripture of Hindus.

* * * * * * * * * * * * * * *

Worksheet 6.1
Taylor Manifest Anxiety Scale

Beside each item below, indicate whether that item is true or false for you.

_____   1.   I do not tire quickly.

_____   2.   I am troubled by attacks of nausea.

_____   3.   I believe I am no more nervous than most others.

_____   4.   I have very few headaches.

_____   5.   I work under a great deal of tension.

_____   6.   I cannot keep my mind on one thing.

_____   7.   I worry over money and business.

_____   8.   I frequently notice my hand shakes when I try
_____   to do something.

_____   9.   I blush no more often than others.

_____   10.   I have diarrhea once a month or more.

_____   11.   I worry quite a bit over possible misfortunes.

_____   12.   I practically never blush.

_____   13.   I am often afraid that I am going to blush.

_____   14.   I have nightmares every few nights.

_____   15.   My hands and feet are usually warm enough.

_____   16.   I sweat very easily even on cool days.

_____   17.   Sometimes when embarrassed, I break out in a
               sweat, which annoys me greatly.

Worksheet 6.1 Taylor Manifest Anxiety Test (Cont'd)

_____ 18.   I hardly ever notice my heart pounding, and I am seldom short of breath.

_____ 19.   I feel hungry almost all the time.

_____ 20.   I am very seldom troubled by constipation.

_____ 21.   I have a great deal of stomach trouble.

_____ 22.   I have had periods in which I lost sleep over worry.

_____ 23.   My sleep is fitful and disturbed.

_____ 24.   I dream frequently about things that are best kept to myself.

_____ 25.   I am easily embarrassed.

_____ 26.   I am more sensitive than most other people.

_____ 27.   I frequently find myself worrying about something.

_____ 28.   I wish I could be as happy as others seem to be.

_____ 29.   I am usually calm and not easily upset.

_____ 30.   I cry easily.

_____ 31.   I feel anxiety about something or someone almost all the time.

_____ 32.   I am happy most of the time.

_____ 33.   It makes me nervous to have to wait.

_____ 34.   I have periods of such great restlessness that I cannot sit long in a chair.

_____ 35.   Sometimes I become so excited that I find it hard to get to sleep.

Worksheet 6.1 Taylor Manifest Anxiety Scale (Cont'd)

_____ 36. I have sometimes felt that difficulties were piling up so high that I could not overcome them.

_____ 37. I must admit that I have at times been worried beyond reason over something that really did not matter.

_____ 38. I have very few fears compared to my friends.

39. I have been afraid of things or people that I know could not hurt me.

_____ 40. I certainly feel useless at times.

_____ 41. I find it hard to keep my mind on a task or job.

_____ 42. I am usually self-conscious.

_____ 43. I am inclined to take things hard.

_____ 44. I am a high-strung person.

_____ 45. Life is a strain for me much of the time.

_____ 46. At times I think I am no good at all.

_____ 47. I am certainly lacking in self-confidence.

_____ 48. I sometimes feel that I am about to go to pieces.

_____ 49. I shrink from facing a crisis or difficulty.

_____ 50. I am entirely self-confident.

FEEDBACK ON WORKSHEET 6.1

To score on this scale let us give ourselves one point for each of the following responses:

1. False	11. True	21. True	31. True	41. True
2. True	12. False	22. True	32. False	42. True
3. False	13. True	23. True	33. True	43. True
4. False	14. True	24. True	34. True	44. True
5. True	15. False	25. True	35. True	45. True
6. True	16. True	26. True	36. True	46. True
7. True	17. True	27. True	37. True	47. True
8. True	18. False	28. True	38. False	48. True
9. False	19. True	29. False	39. True	49. True
10. True	20. False	30. True	40. True	50. False

The average score on this scale is approximately 19. If we scored below that, we feel less anxious than the average person, and if we score above that, we feel more anxious than the average person. If we scored over 35 on this scale, then our anxiety levels are very high and we need to curb this tendency.

* * * * * * * * * * * * * * * *

The Taylor Manifest Anxiety Scale measures what is known as <u>trait anxiety</u>. If our score is over 35 in the Taylor scale, it indicates that our anxiety is evidencing itself in physical and/or psychological symptoms and warrants serious attention (Allen & Hyde, 1980). Therefore, it is necessary for us to master the techniques presented in this chapter. The other type of anxiety is <u>state anxiety</u> which is temporary in nature and is usually associated with a stimulus. This state anxiety is situation specific. The techniques presented in this chapter when practiced over a long time will help in coping with state anxiety also.

Coping Mechanisms

I . <u>Method Based on Rational Emotive Therapy</u> (Dryden & DiGiuseppe, 1990; Ellis, 1971; Ellis, 1975a; Ellis, 1975b; Ellis, 1990; Ellis & Grieger, 1977; Ellis & Harper, 1961; Walen, DiGiuseppe, & Wessler, 1980).

We are constantly engaging in self talk, i.e. the internal thought language by way of which we describe and interpret the world around us. If the beliefs of our self talk are in consonance with reality, then we function well. If the beliefs are irrational and untrue, then this results in stress and emotional disturbance. Ellis's method of Rational Emotive Therapy (R.E.T.) essentially challenges or refutes this very irrational thinking.

In R.E.T., to be rational, we must be (a) practical, (b) logical, (c) objective, and (d) reality-based. On this basis, <u>rationality</u> is an attribute which helps us to achieve our basic goals and purposes in life, be logical, and be consistently aware of reality. On the other hand, <u>irrationality</u> prevents us from achieving our basic goals and purposes, is illogical (especially dogmatic), and is inconsistent with reality. Based upon Rational Emotive Therapy some of the classical irrational ideas are depicted in Thoughts for Reflection 6.2.

Thoughts for Reflection 6.2

Rational Emotive Therapy's 11 Irrational Ideas

1. The idea that it is a dire necessity to be loved or approved by virtually every other significant person.

2. The idea that one should be thoroughly competent, adequate, and achieving in all possible respects if one is to consider oneself worthwhile.

3. The idea that it is certain people are bad, wicked, or villainous and that they should be severely punished and blamed for their villainy.

4. The idea it is awful and catastrophic when things are not the way one would very much like them to be.

5. The idea that human unhappiness is externally controlled, and that people have no ability to control their unhappiness.

6. The idea that something is or may be dangerous or fearsome, one should be concerned about it and should keep dwelling on the possibility of its occurring.

7. The idea that it is easier to avoid than to face certain life difficulties and self responsibilities.

8. The idea that one's past history is an all important determiner of one's present behavior and that because something once strongly affected one's life, it should indefinitely have a similar effect.

9. The idea that one should be dependent on others and need someone stronger than oneself on whom to rely.

10. The idea that one should become quite upset over other people's problems.

11. The idea that there is invariably a right, precise, and perfect solution to human problems, and that is catastrophic if this perfect solution is not found.

Note. From R.E.T. Handbook of Rational Emotive Therapy by A. Ellis and R. Grieger, 1977, New York:, NY: Springer Publishing Company. Copyright 1977 Springer Publishing Company, Inc., New York 10012. Used by permission.

The method based upon R.E.T. is popularly known as the ABCDE technique and consists of five steps:

A. Activating System. This may be either external or internal events which we face. This is also comprised of inferences or interpretations about events around us.

B. Belief System. These are evaluative ideas or constructed views about the world around us. These ideas may either be rigid or flexible. When these beliefs become rigid, they are usually irrational and take the form of "musts," "shoulds," have to's," "got to's," and so on. These beliefs express themselves as:

- "awfulizing," i.e. classifying any situation as 100 percent bad

- "I can't stand it," i.e. low frustration tolerance

- "damnation," i.e. excessively critical of self, others, and/or life conditions

- "always and never thinking," i.e. usage of extreme terms

When our beliefs are flexible, they are rational. These beliefs often take the form of desires, wishes, wants, and preferences. These rational beliefs express themselves as:

- moderate evaluations of badness, e.g. "It is bad, but it is not terrible."

- statements of toleration, e.g. "I don't like it, but I can bear it."

- acceptance of fallibility, e.g. "I was wrong."

- avoidance of extremes, e.g. "Often I do well." (instead of "I always do well.")

C. Consequences. These are emotional and behavioral results about our beliefs. If our beliefs about negative activating events are rigid and irrational then they result in disturbance and are termed inappropriate negative consequences. On the other hand, if our beliefs about negative activating events are flexible and rational, then they do not result in any disturbance and are termed appropriate negative consequences.

D. Dispute Irrational Beliefs. This is the key component needed in order for this method to be effective. If we dispute the irrational beliefs in our mind, then we can also reduce the negative consequences which result.

E. Effect. As a result of disputing the irrational beliefs in our mind, we experience a new and more desirable consequence which is referred to as the effect in this method. Let us now proceed to work through these steps in Worksheet 6.2.

Worksheet 6.2

Anxiety Reduction through R.E.T.

Let us seek out a quiet place and put aside everything else which we have been doing. Now let us follow through the steps detailed below.

Step 1. Activating System

This step entails identifying the stressor. In the space below let us write down the facts of a recent event at the time when we were upset.   Include only objective facts, not conjectures or subjective impressions or value judgements.

_____

_____

_____

Step 2. Belief System

This step entails identifying the rational and irrational beliefs associated with the event. In the space below, let us write down all our judgements, beliefs, assumptions, perceptions, and worries pertaining to the above event.

_____

_____

_____

Step 3. Consequences

Let us identify the physical, mental, and behavioral results. Let us try to present this in the form of a summary word(s), e.g. anger, grief.

_____

_____

_____

Worksheet 6.2 Anxiety Reduction through R.E.T. (Cont'd)

Step 4. **Dispute Irrational Beliefs**

    i. Let us select <u>one</u> irrational belief at a time.

_____

    ii. Is there any rational support for this idea? Our response needs to be **"NO."**

    iii. Let us assign reasons for this falseness.

_____

_____

    iv. What is the worst that can happen according to this irrational idea?

_____

_____

    v. What are the good things that can happen if we do not accept this irrational idea?

_____

_____

Step 5. **Effect**

    Let us prepare for the worst events which can happen if we accept this irrational belief. Let us focus on the benefits which can occur if you do not accept this irrational belief. Let us give autosuggestions (self-talk) to refute this irrational belief. As a consequence of this new thinking, we will experience the positive results. Let us proceed in a similar fashion with other irrational ideas and practice this technique regularly.

* * * * * * * * * * * * * * *

II. __Method Based on Simplified Kundalini Yoga (SKY)__ (Maharishi, 1989).

This method, derived from Indian philosophy, is based on the principles of introspection as advocated by Yogiraj Vethathiri Maharishi, a contemporary philosopher and teacher from India who has formed the World Community Service Center which has branches all over the world (See Chapter 3). This method entails the following steps:

__Step 1__. We need to seek a quiet place, have availability of at least one half hour of uninterrupted time, and have a sheet of paper and pencil with us.

__Step 2__. This step involves thinking, contemplating, and compiling a list of all the worries that are bothering us at the present time.

__Step 3__. In this step we classify the worries into four types:

(1) __Worries that should be faced__. For example, a child is born with a birth defect (congenital anomaly). Despite all the best efforts, he or she cannot be cured by any medicine or other means. How can we solve this worry? What is the use of brooding over such a worry? Therefore, in order to manage such worries, we need to resolve with ourselves that there is no use worrying over things over which we have no control. Make your mind firm and abide by this resolution. In this category worries like chronic diseases, loss of property, and death will be listed.

(2) __Worries to be solved immediately__. These are the worries which have to be dealt with immediately and boldly. For example, one such worry is about general illness. It can be managed immediately by resorting to proper medication, diet, and life-style changes.
Similarly, such worries can arise out of differences of opinion in the family. We cannot disown our families, therefore, these worries need be managed by mutual discussion without any delay. Other worries about poverty and debts can be managed by hard work, perseverance, and economy in spending.

(3) __Worries that may be postponed__. For example, consider a person who has reached attained an age suitable for marriage and is not able to find the right partner. For tackling such a worry, he or she has to keep on trying patiently and allow time to take its course. Therefore, action on such a worry can be postponed.

(4) __Worries to be ignored__. For example, your boss has a habit of constantly nagging you with his/her outmoded ideas and notions. The best thing to do in such a situation would be to quietly keep on doing your best, unmindful of the purposeless advice given to you. In this category, worries arising out of differences of opinion, jealousy, etc. will be listed.

__Step 4__. Having classified all our worries into the above four types, the total number of worries to be tackled at the present time will be decreased. This will reduce an unnecessary burden on our mind. Do not think that there will be no more worries in the future or that these worries will completely cease to exist? After one worry is resolved, another one will "spring up." After we climb one mountain, another peak will come into our vision to be conquered. But what we can do now is work in a planned way to reduce our worries. Worksheet 6.3 helps us to classify our worries according to this method in order to lessen the burden on our mind.

Worksheet 6.3
Anxiety Reduction through SKY

Let us seek out a quiet place for at least one half hour to contemplate.
Let us think about and compile our worries into the following categories:

Worries to be faced	Worries to be solved immediately	Worries to be postponed	Worries to be ignored

Note. From "Yoga for modern age" (3rd ed.) by Y.V. Maharishi, 1989, Madras, India: Vethathiri Publications. Copyright 1989 by Y. V. Maharishi. Reprinted by permission.

FEEDBACK ON WORKSHEET 6.3

Classification of our worries bothering our mind at the present moment into the four categories must have resulted in reducing the total number of worries to be tackled at the <u>present</u> time. This will reduce an unnecessary burden on our mind. In this way whenever our mind is flooded with a number of worries and problems, we can sit down and practice this technique to reduce the total number of worries at any time. This is a useful and effective approach which conserves our energy that can be used for other productive activities.

* * * * * * * * * * * * * * * *

III. **Method Based on Gestalt Therapy** (Corey 1991; Corsini, 1984; Perls, 1969)

Gestalt is a German word meaning whole or configuration (Simkin, 1976). As one psychological dictionary puts it, Gestalt is ". . . an integration of the whole as contrasted with summation of parts." (Warren, 1934). The originator of Gestalt Therapy, Fredrick S. Perls drew out an analogy of the concept of this theory with an organism which always works as a whole. Organisms are not a summation of parts but a coordination of organ systems or other components (Perls, 1969). Gestalt Therapy emphasizes the unity of self awareness behavior and experience. The goal of Gestalt Therapy is to help us get in touch with reality and focus on the "now." It implicitly asks individuals to accept that they will be more comfortable and effective in their lives in the long run if they are fully aware of what they are doing from moment to moment and accept responsibility for their behaviors. By discovering <u>what is</u> rather than what should be or what could have been, or the ideal of what should be or may be, the person learns to trust himself or herself. A Gestalt prayer summarizes this philosophy:

> *I do my thing, and you do your thing.*
> *I am not in this world to live up to your expectations*
> *And you are not in this world to live up to mine.*
> *You are you, and I am I,*
> *And if by chance we find each other, it's beautiful.*
> *If not, it can't be helped.*

A modified process based on the principles of this Gestalt Therapy is provided in Worksheet 6.4 for you to practice.

IV. <u>Systematic Desensitization</u>

This technique was first described by Joseph Wolpe (1958, 1971) and involves imagining or experiencing an anxiety-provoking scene while practicing a response incompatible with anxiety (such as relaxation). This concept is also utilized in the field of medicine for treating allergies. The allergic patient is exposed to very small doses of allergen which are gradually increased till the body learns to accept the allergen. In coping with anxiety also, the basic method entails slow and steady adjustments to small components of any problem. Each small step is considered one at a time and relaxation is practiced alongside to counteract the adverse response. This technique involves developing a fear hierarchy, which is a sequence of small steps that lead to the anxiety-provoking event. Let us consider an example. Suppose we are students and we have test anxiety. Our fear hierarchy would be as follows:

1. Enrolling for the course
2. Going to the classes
3. Completing the assignments
4. Studying the textbook
5. Studying additional materials
6. Reviewing the text
7. Preparing for examinations
8. Going to the examination
9. Waiting before the examination
10. Taking the examination
11. Waiting for the results of the examination
12. Obtaining the results

Most of the test anxiety is tied into the <u>expectations</u> of obtaining a good result, and therefore, we have included that dimension in the fear hierarchy. Similarly we can construct fear hierarchy for any fear that causes us anxiety. This procedure has been described systematically in a stepwise fashion in Worksheet 6.5 for you to practice.

Worksheet 6.4
Coping with Anxiety Based on Gestalt Therapy

Let us follow the steps below and write down our responses wherever needed:

Step 1.   Let us seek out a quiet place and focus our awareness on our thinking.

Step 2.   Let us write down what thoughts are coming into our mind and at the same time be consciously aware of our body movements, if any.

Thoughts:

_____

_____

_____

_____

_____

_____

_____

_____

_____

_____

_____

_____

_____

Worksheet 6.4 Coping with Anxiety Based on Gestalt Therapy (Cont'd)

Body movements/ sensations during thoughts:

_____

_____

_____

_____

Step 3.   Let us list the painful thoughts which we do not want to come into our mind.

_____

_____

_____

_____

Step 4.   Let us experience the pain associated with the above thoughts with awareness rather than alleviating it. If painful thoughts become too overbearing, then we must stop and relax.

FEEDBACK ON WORKSHEET 6.4.

Let us try to establish consonance between our thoughts and body movements. If we are not able to derive any inferences do not worry and proceed. Let us practice this awareness-building exercise and ALWAYS FOCUS ON NOW , i.e. the thoughts that are arising at this moment in time. If painful thoughts become too overbearing, then we must stop and relax. This can be practiced individually or in groups. With regular practice our skills in coping with anxiety will increase.

* * * * * * * * * * * * * * *

Worksheet 6.5
Systematic Desensitization

We need to proceed according to the steps mentioned below:

Step 1.   Let us seek a quiet, comfortable, and peaceful place. Let us select a relaxation technique described in Chapter 3 and relax. Let us write down the name of this technique below:

_____

Let us print the word "relax" below.

_____

Step 2.   Let us develop a fear hierarchy for the fear which causes us anxiety. Write down all the small steps leading to that fear. We need to have a minimum of 10 steps.

Fear: _____

Hierarchy:

(i)   _____

(ii)   _____

(iii)   _____

(iv)   _____

(v)   _____

(vi)   _____

(vii)   _____

(viii) _____

(ix)   _____

Worksheet 6.5 Systematic Desensitization (Cont'd)

(x)   _____

_____

_____

_____

_____

Step 3.   Let us relax.

Step 4.   Let us imagine the first item in the fear hierarchy list for one to five seconds. We need to gradually increase the thinking time to about a minute.

Step 5.   Let us relax.

Step 6.   We need to repeat Step 4 on the next item. If we have difficulty with any item, let us break it down further into smaller steps and approach it gradually in our mind. We need to reassure ourselves that there is nothing to fear.

FEEDBACK ON WORKSHEET 6.5

With regular practice of this technique, we will be able to get over our fear and reduce anxiety when we encounter that event. In this way we will be able to strengthen our mind and not be bogged down by small fears.

* * * * * * * * * * * * * *

Let us practice all the techniques described in this chapter and find the one that is best for us. We need to keep practicing that technique for best results. We may want to change from one technique to the other over time or we may want to practice the same technique. The approach will vary from one person to the other.

Stress Management Principle # 6

We need to wipe out anxiety before it wipes us out.

Summary Points

- Anxiety arises out of inefficiency and fear.

- Excessive anxiety is associated with Generalized Anxiety Disorder and Panic Disorder.

- Taylor Manifest Anxiety Scale measures Trait Anxiety.

- Rational Emotive Therapy (R.E.T.) based ABCDE technique described by Albert Ellis consists of five steps: Identifying the Activating System, Identifying the Belief System, Identifying the Consequences, Disputing Irrational Beliefs, and Visualizing the Effects.

- Coping with anxiety using Simplified Kundalini Yoga as described by Yogiraj Vethathiri Maharishi consists of classifying worries into those to be faced, those to be solved immediately, those to be postponed, and those to be ignored.

- Coping with anxiety using Gestalt Therapy described by Fredrick Perls helps us to focus on the "now," discovering "what is reality," and bearing the pain, if any.

- Systematic Desensitization described by Joseph Wolpe involves analyzing any anxiety provoking situation in terms of smaller steps and counteracting those steps at each stage by practicing relaxation.

References and Further Readings

Allen, R.J., & Hyde, D. (1980). Investigations in stress control. Minneapolis, MN: Burgess Publishing Company.

Corey, G. (1991). Theory and practice of counseling and psychotherapy. Pacific Grove, CA: Brooks/Cole.

Corsini, R.J. (1984). Current psychotherapies. (3rd ed.). Itasca, IL: Peacock Publishers, Inc.

Diagnostic and statistical manual of mental disorders. (4th ed. rev.). (DSM IV). (1994). Washington D.C.: American Psychiatric Association.

Dryden, W. & DiGiuseppe, R. (1990). A primer on rational emotive therapy. Champaign, Illinois: Research Press.

Ellis, A., & Harper, R. (1961). A guide to rational living. North Hollywood, CA: Willshire Books.

Ellis, A. (1971). Growth through reason. Palo Alto, CA: Science & Behavior Books.

Ellis, A. (1975a). A new guide to rational living. North Hollywood, CA: Willshire Books.

Ellis, A. (1975b). How to live with a neurotic at home and at work. (Rev. ed.). North Hollywood, CA: Willshire Books.

Ellis, A. & Grieger, R. (1977). RET Handbook of rational emotive therapy. New York, NY: Springer Publishing Company.

Ellis, A. (1990). How to stubbornly refuse to make yourself miserable about anything - yes anything. New York, NY: Carol Publishing Group.

Greenberg, J.S. (1993). Comprehensive stress management. (4th ed.). Dubuque, IA: William C. Brown Publishers.

Maharishi, Y.V. (1989). Yoga for modern age. (3rd ed.). Madras, India: Vethathiri Publications.

Perls, F.S. (1969). Gestalt Therapy Verbatim. Moab, UT: Real People Press.

Regier, D.A., Boyd J.H., Burke, J.D. Jr. et al. (1988). One month prevalence of mental disorders in the United States: Based on five epidemiological catchment area studies. Archives of General Psychiatry, 45, 977-986.

References and Further Readings (Cont'd)

Shader, R.I. & Greenblatt, D.J. (1993). Use of Benzodiazepines in anxiety disorders. The New England Journal of Medicine, 328, 1398-1405.

Simkin, J.S. (1976). Gestalt therapy. Mini lectures. Millbrae, CA: Celestial Arts.

Walen, S.R., DiGiuseppe, R., & Wessler, R.L. (1980). A practitioner's guide to rational emotive therapy. New York, NY: Oxford University Press.

Warren, H.D. (1934). Dictionary of Psychology. New York, NY: Houghton Mifflin & Company.

Wolpe, J. (1958). Psychotherapy by reciprocal inhibition. Stanford, CA: Stanford University Press.

Wolpe, J. (1973). The practice of behavior therapy. (2nd ed.). New York, NY: Pergamon.

CHAPTER 7

BALANCED DIET AND APPROPRIATE EATING

Bien haya el que invento el sueno,
capa que cubre todos los humanos pensanientos,
manjar que quita la hambre,
agua que ahuyenta la sed,
fuego que calienta el frio,
frio que templa el ardor, y, finalmente,
momeda general conque todas las cosas se compran,
balnza y peso que iguala al pastor con el rey
y al simple con el discreto.

[Blessings on him who invented sleep,
the mantle that covers all human thoughts,
the food that satisfies hunger,
the drink that slakes thirst,
the fire that warms cold,
the cold that moderates heat, and, lastly,
the common currency that buys all things,
the balance and weight that equalizes the shepherd
*   and the King*
the simpleton and the sage.]

Miguel De Cervantes

Importance of Balanced Diet and Appropriate Eating

Belloc and Breslow (1972), after surveying nearly 7000 individuals identified seven behaviors related to the maintenance of personal health:

1. Sleeping seven to eight hours daily.

2. Eating breakfast almost daily.

3. Consuming planned snacks.

4. Being at or near prescribed weight (gender & height specific)

5. Never smoking cigarettes.

6. Moderate or no use of alcohol.

7. Regular physical activity.

While the exact role and mechanism of each of these factors has not been completely understood, it has generally been accepted that all these factors contribute significantly toward maintaining health and longevity. In this chapter we shall primarily be focusing on diet and related eating behaviors. The importance of eating nutritious meals appropriately plays a significant role in healthy living, helps combat daily stress, and also reduces undue stress. Though the relationship between diet and stress has not been studied extensively (Greenberg, 1993), the importance of eating a balanced diet to maintain health and reduce stress cannot be ruled out (Girdano, Everly, & Dusek, 1993). Consumption of a healthy balanced diet enhances our coping abilities against various stressors and stressful events. When our meals consist of all the ingredients of a balanced diet, then our body has sufficient energy in coping with stress. A balanced diet also provides enough reserves to manage stress. Irregular eating of meals, eating improper food (that is, undercooked or overcooked, too spicy or too bland, consisting of only one category of food, stale food, unpalatable food, and so on), undereating or overeating unduly taxes the body and is a potential source of stress in itself. If we eat these meals after sufficient appetite has set in, and do not indulge in overeating, then the body is saved from undue stress and associated negative consequences. On the other hand, undereating also creates stress for the body because enough energy is not available to perform daily activities. Therefore, the key lies in maintaining **balance** with quantity and quality of food and regularity in eating.

Enhancing Awareness about Our Dietary Patterns

How well do we eat? Is our diet balanced? Do we eat our meals regularly? These are some of the questions about which we may not be able to answer impromptu. The reason is that most of us have become quite used to eating food daily. We seldom take time to think about what we eat and how we eat. We have taken eating for granted. We need to become aware about our diet and eating patterns and consider a change. This awareness about our diet and eating patterns is a central and important step in effecting a change in our behavior. Therefore, before we proceed any further, let us become more aware about our own dietary habits and patterns with the help of Worksheet 7.1.

Worksheet 7.1
Enhancing Awareness about Diet and Eating

Let us think and respond to the following items in order to obtain feedback regarding our dietary habits and patterns:

1. Height   _____

2. Weight   _____

3. What weight is appropriate for me?   _____

4. When was the last time that I recorded my weight?

   _____

5. How often do I record my weight?

   _____ Daily
   _____ Weekly
   _____ Fortnightly
   _____ Monthly
   _____ Bimonthly
   _____ Quarterly
   _____ Yearly
   _____ Whenever you feel like
   _____ Sometimes, irregularly
   _____ Never

6. Do I eat breakfast?

   _____ Regularly every day
   _____ Occasionally
   _____ Never

7. Do I eat between meals?

   _____ Always
   _____ Occasionally
   _____ Never

Worksheet 7.1 Enhancing Awareness About Diet And Eating (Cont'd)

8. Do I drink coffee, tea or colas?

_____ Everyday   What type? _____

                         How much? _____

_____ Occasionally What type? _____

                         How much? _____

_____ Never

9. Do I smoke tobacco products?

_____ Everyday   What type? _____

                         How much? _____

_____ Occasionally What type? _____

                         How much? _____

_____ Never

10. Do I drink alcoholic beverages?

_____ Everyday   What type? _____

                         How much? _____

_____ Occasionally What type? _____

                         How much? _____

_____ Never

11. Do I take any illegal drugs?

_____ Yes   What type? _____

                         How much? _____

_____ No

Worksheet 7.1 Enhancing Awareness about Diet and Eating (Cont'd)

12. Let us put a check mark beside those food items which I eat at least once per day:

    ____ Canned foods
    ____ Processed Cheese
    ____ Seasonings
    ____ Sausage/Ham/Bacon (Red Meat)
    ____ Chips (Potato/Corn/Tortilla)
    ____ Table salt
    ____ Pizza
    ____ "Fast foods"

13. How often do I eat chocolate?

    ____ Never
    ____ Rarely
    ____ Often
    ____ Sometimes
    ____ Daily

14. What is my level of sugar consumption (namely; candy)?

    ____ Excessive
    ____ Moderate
    ____ Adequate
    ____ Less than Normal

FEEDBACK ON WORKSHEET 7.1

Items 1 - 3. Ideal weight depends upon gender, height and build. Information about ideal weight based upon height, body frame and gender is depicted on Table 7-1 on the following page. In order to check our ideal weight, we need to first assess our build. Then find out our height and look for the range of our weight in the table which follows.

FEEDBACK ON WORKSHEET 7.1 (Cont'd)

Table 7-1 Weight Chart

M E N
Acceptable Weight (lbs. without clothing)

Height	Small Frame	Medium Frame	Large Frame
5'1"	123-129	126-136	133-145
5'2"	125-131	128-138	135-148
5'3"	127-133	130-140	137-151
5'4"	129-135	132-143	139-155
5'5"	131-137	134-146	141-159
5'6"	133-140	137-149	144-163
5'7"	135-143	140-152	147-167
5'8"	137-146	143-155	150-171
5'9"	139-149	146-158	153-175
5'10"	141-152	149-161	156-179
5'11"	144-155	152-165	159-183
6'0"	147-159	155-169	163-187
6'1"	150-163	159-173	167-192
6'2"	153-167	162-177	171-197
6'3"	157-171	166-182	176-202

W O M E N
Acceptable Weight (lbs. without clothing)

Height	Small Frame	Medium Frame	Large Frame
4'9"	99-108	106-118	115-128
4'10"	100-110	108-120	117-131
4'11"	101-112	110-123	119-134
5'0"	103-115	112-126	122-137
5'1"	105-118	115-129	125-140
5'2"	108-121	118-132	128-144
5'3"	111-124	121-135	131-148
5'4"	114-127	124-138	134-152
5'5"	117-130	127-141	137-156
5'6"	120-133	130-144	140-160
5'7"	123-136	133-147	143-164
5'8"	126-139	136-150	146-167
5'9"	129-142	139-153	149-170
5'10"	132-145	142-156	152-173
5'11"	135-148	145-159	155-176

Note. From The American Medical Association Family Medical Guide , p. 28, by American Medical Association. Copyright © 1982 by The American Medical Association. Reprinted by Permission of Random House, Inc.

FEEDBACK ON WORKSHEET 7.1 (Cont'd)

<u>Items 4 - 5</u>. We need to maintain our weight based upon the ideal range for our height, body frame and gender. Therefore, we should record our weight regularly. A written record provides us with a chronological baseline to compare and make changes as necessary. However, this does not mean that we be fanatic about recording weights too often because weight changes are slow to occur. It is good if we record weight fortnightly or monthly.

<u>Item 6</u>. Research indicates that hypoglycemia or low blood sugar predisposes an individual to stress. Symptoms of hypoglycemia may include anxiety, headache, dizziness, trembling, and increased cardiac activity (Girdano, Everly & Dusek, 1993). The best way to avoid stress associated with hypoglycemia, for a normal person, is to eat a balanced breakfast everyday.

<u>Item 7</u>. Eating continuously in between meals unduly activates the digestive system, leading to a release of various chemicals and byproducts which may add to the stress getting built up. This self-induced stress can be controlled by planning to consume food more appropriately.

<u>Item 8</u>. Coffee, Tea, and Colas have <u>caffeine</u> which is identified as a sympathomimetic agent or a pseudostressor. When consumed, they trigger a stress response in the body. A six-ounce cup of coffee (Coffea arabica) contains about 108 milligrams of caffeine, Tea (Camelia theca) contains 90 mg/cup. Various cola beverages contain 50-60 mg/12oz. and a bar of chocolate (1 oz.) about 20 mg (Girdano, Everly, Dusek, 1993).

<u>Item 9</u>. Nicotine found in tobacco is also a sympathomimetic agent and produces a stress response in the body. Tobacco smoke also contains various other harmful products such as tar and carbon monoxide which can lead to bronchitis, lung cancer and other diseases.

<u>Item 10</u>. Alcohol is a Central Nervous System inhibitor although it may appear to reduce stress. However, stress is known to be tied to alcohol addiction (Schlaadt, 1992). There are approximately 10 to 13 million alcoholics in the United States and more than 7 million alcohol abusers. Alcohol abuse is at the root of impaired job performance, child abuse, spouse abuse, accidental injuries, and medical disorders (Seventh Special Report to the U.S. Congress on Alcohol & Health, 1990).

FEEDBACK ON WORKSHEET 7.1 (Cont'd)

Item 11. Illegal drugs may be grouped into <u>five categories</u>: <u>stimulants</u>, like cocaine; marijuana and its derivatives; <u>depressants</u>, such as the opiates; <u>psyche-delics</u>; <u>deliriants</u>; and "<u>designer drugs</u>" (Donatelle & Davis, 1993). These drugs do not relieve stress. In fact they add to the stress response in the long run. Adopting these negative mechanisms for temporary relief of stress can be extremely hazardous and ruin our physical, mental, and social well-being.

Item 12. Fast foods and other products mentioned in the list are rich in <u>sodi-um</u> content. Sodium is a mineral responsible for regulating water balance in the body. The United States Recommended Dietary Allowances suggest no more than 2400 milligrams (mg) of sodium per day. If the products which you have checked are high in sodium, it is important that we restrict their usage. A good nutritious diet provides the necessary sodium and excessive sodium may contribute to an increase in blood pressure and stress (Greenberg, 1993).

Item 13. Chocolate contains <u>caffeine</u> and <u>sugar</u>. Caffeine, as explained earlier, is a pseudostressor or a sympathomimetic agent. This induces a response in the body which is akin to the stress response. Excess sugar provides the body with unused energy and this usually leads to the accumulation of harmful byproducts. Both these products therefore add to our stress and need to be avoided.

Item 14. Excessive sugar, as has been explained above, leaves excess unused energy in the body. This does not relieve stress, but in fact adds to our stress levels. Moreover, consuming large quantities of sugar over a long period may contribute to weight gain and various diseases directly or indirectly, such as diabetes mellitus. Therefore, it is best to regulate the intake of sugar in our diets.

* * * * * * * * * * * * * *

Different Categories of Food Items

Let us briefly understand the various types of food items and what they do to our body. The various food items can be classified, from a nutrition point of view, into the following six categories:

1. __Carbohydrates__: Carbohydrate is a word of Chemistry. Chemically, the word "carbohydrate" is derived from "carbo" implying carbon and "hydrate" implying hydrogen and oxygen. That is, these compounds are constituted of varying proportions of carbon, hydrogen, and oxygen. Food items rich in carbohydrates include sugars, bread (wheat flour), fibrous lining of fruits and vegetables, cereals, rice, pasta (wheat flour), roots and tubers and so on. These food items when consumed and digested provide the body with **energy**. This energy helps the body perform its daily activities. They also provide the diet with fiber, which adds to the bulk and facilitate easy elimination from the bowel. It is important to consume these vital categories of food products in **moderation**. If too little carbohydrates are consumed, then the body does not get enough energy to perform daily tasks. If they are ingested in excess, the body tends to convert and store these products for future use. If this excess carbohydrate persists for a long time and is at the cost of other vital food items, then fat deposition and other health-related problems occur. Further, if our diet solely consists of carbohydrates, then the body is deprived of other vital categories of food items and the body is weakened, especially in coping with long-term demands of stress. Thus the importance of using moderation and combining this category with other food categories cannot be overemphasized. Determining the correct amount of carbohydrates to be consumed is dependent upon many factors including the amount of daily activity, type of activities, body constitution, and so on. As a general rule, 6-11 servings of grain products are recommended per day by the U.S. Department of Agriculture (See Figure 7-1). If our activity levels are more sedentary in nature or if our body constitution is smaller, we may stick to the lower limit of the prescribed range for observing moderation. Use of sugars per se needs to be curtailed. Thoughts for Reflection 7.1 provide us with some suggestions.

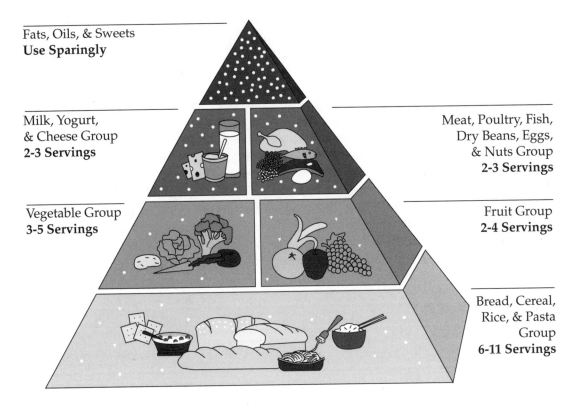

Figure 7-1 Food Pyramid

<u>Note</u>. From U. S. Department of Agriculture

Thoughts for Reflection 7.1

Using Sugars in Moderation - Some Suggestions

At the Supermarket:

- Read ingredient labels. Identify all the added sugars in a product. Select items lower in added sugars when possible.

- Buy fresh fruits or fruits packed in water or juice, rather than those in light or heavy syrup.

- Buy fewer foods that are high in sugars such as soft drinks, fruit flavored punches and sweet desserts. Be aware that some low fat desserts may be very high in sugars.

In the Kitchen:

- Reduce the sugars in foods you prepare at home. Try new recipes or make your own. Start by reducing sugars gradually until you have decreased them by one-third or more.

- Experiment with spices such as cinnamon, cardamom, coriander, nutmeg, ginger, and mace to enhance the sweet flavor of foods. Spiced foods will taste sweeter if warmed.

- When possible, use home-prepared items (made with less sugars) instead of commercially prepared ones that are higher in sugars.

At the Table:

- Use less of all sugars including white and brown sugars, honey, molasses, syrups, jams, and jellies.

- Choose fewer foods that are high in added sugars such as prepared baked goods, candies, and sweet desserts.

- Reach for fresh fruit instead of something sweetened with additional sugars for dessert or a snack.

- Add less sugars to foods - coffee, tea, cereal, or fruit. Get used to using half as much, then see if you can cut back even more.

- Cut back on the number of sugar-sweetened soft drinks, punches, and ades you drink.

Note. From Use sugars only in moderation (p. 5) by United States Department of Agriculture (Human Nutrition Information Service), July 1993, Washington D.C.: U.S. Government Printing Office. Material under Public domain.

2. Proteins: The word "protein" is derived from the Greek word *Proteios* meaning prime or chief. Proteins are in fact the most important constituents of our diet. There are two major sources of dietary proteins: (a) <u>animal sources</u>: eggs, milk, meat, fish and so on, (b) <u>plant sources</u>: lentils, cereals, nuts, beans, and so on. The prime function of protein is **body building**. Proteins are needed for growth, maintenance, and replacement of body cells. They are also required in the production of most hormones and enzymes which regulate the body functioning. In order to combat stress, they are important constituents. If the diet lacks enough proteins, then the body becomes emaciated and stress-fighting capabilities are also substantially reduced. Extreme environmental or physiological stresses increase nitrogen loss through urine and increase energy expenditure (Cuthberston, 1964). This necessitates the need for greater amounts of protein intake. On the other hand, if the diet contains excess protein, then they are converted to carbohydrates and stored for future use. If this excess persists, then that is also not good for the body. It may lead to unwanted and unused byproducts which are potentially harmful to the body. Some proteins are also responsible for allergic manifestations in many susceptible people. Therefore, a **moderation** in intake of proteins is essential. According to U.S. Department of Health and Nutrition, 2-3 servings from milk, yogurt, and cheese group; and meat, poultry, fish, dry beans, eggs and nuts group per day are recommended (See Figure 7-1).

3. Fats: Fats are sources of energy and are important in helping to carry some vitamins (fat soluble vitamins). Some fats also form cell membranes and hormones. They also add flavor to foods. Dietary fats are derived from two sources: (a) <u>animal sources</u>: butter, lard, and so on, and (b) <u>plant sources</u>: various edible oils like sunflower, canola, olive, and so on. Fats should be used **sparingly** in the diet. As explained earlier, small quantities of fat are required by the body for performing some vital functions. However, when taken in excess, they tend to accumulate in the body. Excess deposition of fats leads to obesity which has been associated as a risk factor for a number of disorders including coronary heart disease, stroke and so on. Thoughts for Reflection 7.2 provide some suggestions for reducing cholesterol and fats in the diet.

Thoughts for Reflection 7.2

Easy Ways to Cut Fat, Saturated Fat, and Cholesterol in Your Diet

At the Store:

- Choose lean cuts of meat, such as beef round, loin, sirloin, pork loinchops, and roasts.

- Consider fish and poultry as alternatives; they are somewhat lower in saturated fat.

- Buy low fat versions of dairy products.

- Read the food label and choose foods that are lower in fat, saturated fat, and cholesterol.

In the Kitchen:

- When cooking, replace saturated fats, such as butter and lard, with small amounts of polyunsaturated and monounsaturated fats in vegetable oils such as corn oil, soybean oil, olive oil, peanut oil, or canola oil.

- Broil, roast, bake, steam, or boil foods instead of frying them, or try stirfrying with just a little fat.

- Trim all visible fat from meat before it is cooked.

- Spoon off fat from meat dishes after they are cooked.

- Use skim milk or low fat milk when making "cream" sauces, soups or puddings.

- Substitute low fat yogurt or whipped low fat cottage cheese for sour cream and mayonnaise in dips and dressings.

- Substitute two egg whites for each whole egg in recipes for most quick breads, cookies, and cakes (The cholesterol and fat are in the yolk, not in the white).

- Try lemon juice, herbs, or spices to season foods instead of butter or margarine.

Thoughts for Reflection 7.2 Easy Ways to Cut Fat, Saturated fat, and Cholesterol in Your Diet (Cont'd)

<u>At the Table</u>:

- Use less of **all** fats and oils, especially saturated fats such as butter, cream, sour cream, and cream cheese.

- Try reduced-calorie salad dressings-they are usually low in fat.

- As a beverage, gradually replace whole milk with 2 percent fat milk, then 1 percent fat or skim milk.

Note. From <u>Food facts for older adults. Information on how to use the dietary guidelines</u> (p. 6) by Human Nutrition Information Service, U.S. Department of Agriculture and National Institute on Aging, National Institutes of Health, 1993, Hyattsville, MD: United States Department of Agriculture. Material under Public domain.

---

4. <u>Vitamins</u>: The word "vitamin" is derived from the earlier German word *vitamine* (*vita* meaning life, and *amine* based on the earlier notion that all these substances contained amino acids chemically). These are substances which are needed by the body in extremely small amounts. Though vitamins do not supply energy directly, they do help in the release of energy from other substances and play an important role in completing many chemical reactions within the body. Vitamins can be broadly classified into two types: (a) <u>fat soluble</u>: A, D, E, and K; and (b) <u>water soluble</u>: B, and C. Some of the key sources of different vitamins are depicted in Table 7-3 below.

Table 7-3   Important Sources of Some Vitamins

Vitamin	Sources
A (Retinol)	Egg, whole milk, fish, green leafy vegetables like spinach, cabbage, broccoli; colored vegetables like carrots and pumpkin; fruits like papaya
B_1 (Thiamine)	Dried yeast, unmilled cereals, lentils, nuts and oilseeds
B_2 (Riboflavin)	Liver, meat, milk, eggs, germinating lentils, cereals, and vegetables
Niacin	Grain products; and milk, eggs (contain tryptophan which can be converted to niacin)
B_6 (Pyridoxine)	Chicken, fish, kidney, liver, pork, eggs, unmilled rice, soy beans, oats, whole wheat products, peanuts, and walnuts
Folic Acid	Liver, yeast, leafy vegetables, legumes, and some fruits
B_{12}	Liver, meat, eggs, milk
C (Ascorbic Acid)	Green and red peppers, collard greens, broccoli, spinach, tomatoes, potatoes, strawberries, oranges, and other citrus fruits
D	Sunlight; fortified milk, fortified margarine, eggs, butter
E	Vegetable oils (soy bean, corn, cottonseed, safflower)
K	Green leafy vegetables, milk, meats, eggs, cereals, fruits and vegetables

If fat-soluble vitamins are consumed in excess, they tend to accumulate in the body which is responsible for disorders called hypervitaminosis. There is general consensus that these vitamins should not be taken in excess as supplements. Water-soluble vitamins, if taken in excess, are easily excreted out of the system. However, authorities are divided on recommending their excess use. While some believe they cause no harm, others believe that they can be harmful too (like formation of renal stones by taking excess Vitamin C). We would recommend a balance in taking vitamins. From a stress management point of view, vitamins are essential in optimum quantities for maintaining the body's resistance to stress.

5. <u>Minerals</u>: Minerals are also needed in relatively small amounts. They are primarily needed to make hemoglobin in red blood cells and strengthen bones and teeth. They are also essential to maintain body fluids and chemical reactions in the body. They improve the body's capability in managing stress more effectively if taken in **optimum** quantities. Some of the important minerals helpful in combating stress are calcium, iron, zinc and magnesium. Another important consideration with respect to minerals is to reduce the intake of common salt (sodium chloride) in the diet. High intake of common salt induces retention of body fluids and elicits the stress response. Thoughts for Reflection 7.3 provide us with some ideas for reducing sodium in our diets.

Thoughts for Reflection 7.3

Some Tips on Reducing Sodium in Your Diet

<u>At the Store</u>:

- Read labels for information on the sodium content.

- Try fresh or plain frozen vegetables and meats instead of those canned or prepared with salt.

- Look for low or reduced sodium or "no-salt-added" versions of foods.

<u>In the Kitchen</u>:

- Cook plain rice, pasta, and hot cereals using less salt than the package calls for (try 1/8 teaspoon of salt for two servings). "Instant" rice, pasta, and cereals may contain salt added by the processor.

- Adjust your recipes, gradually cutting down on the amount of salt. If some of the ingredients already contain salt, such as canned soup or vegetables, you may need to add no more salt at all.

- Use herbs and spices as seasonings for vegetables and meats instead of salt.

<u>At the table</u>:

- Taste your food before you salt it. Does it really need more salt? Try one shake instead of two. Gradually cut down on the amount of salt you use. Your taste will adjust to less salt.

<u>Note</u>. From <u>Food facts for older adults. Information on how to use the dietary guidelines</u> (p. 8-9) by Human Nutrition Information Service, U.S. Department of Agriculture and National Institute on Aging, National Institutes of Health, 1993, Hyattsville, MD: United States Department of Agriculture. Material under Public domain.

* * * * * * * * * * * * * *

6. Water: This extremely important constituent of the diet is most often forgotten. We take it for granted most of the time. In the absence of water life will perish. Water helps to transport all the body nutrients, removes waste products and regulates body temperature. In order to effectively combat stress, the body needs an adequate supply of water. Water also helps to dilute the harmful chemical substances if they are accumulating in the body. Water also helps in excretion of these substances. It is recommended that we drink 8-10 glasses of water every day. This means that water should be consumed at times when one is not even thirsty. It also means that we should not replace water with other beverages, soft drinks, and so on. We have already seen that most beverages, like cola, tea, coffee, etc. contain caffeine and other preservatives which do more harm than good. Hence water is the only constituent of the diet which, for the most part, does no harm to the body and has only beneficial results. We would like to suggest that one consume as much water as possible.

Avoiding Alcohol, Smoking and Drug Abuse

The issues of alcohol and drug abuse are extensive and complex in nature. However, we would like to briefly discuss some points regarding these issues here because many people resort to finding solutions to their stress by using, misusing, and abusing chemical substances.

Drinking alcoholic beverages is associated with a number of health problems. Alcoholic beverages supply calories to the body but fail to provide any nutrients. These "empty calories" often lead to malnourishment and decreased capabilities in combating daily stresses. Excessive alcohol use has also been associated as a risk factor with cirrhosis of liver, inflammation of the pancreas, damage to the brain and heart, and increased risk for a variety of cancers. Alcohol is a Central Nervous System depressant and therefore, decreases reaction time, hampers judgement, and impairs sensory responses. As we have already seen in Chapters 1 and 2, perception of a stressor is central to effectively manage stress. When this perception is distorted by use of alcohol, recuperation from stress is considerably lowered.

Many of us smoke in order to get relief from stress. However, this is not true. Tobacco smoke contains nicotine which is a pseudostressor as we have already seen in the Worksheet 7.1. When the body gets habituated to smoking, it requires more nicotine to get the release of normal chemicals, which may falsely give a smoker the feeling of getting relief from stress. This stress is in fact self-inflicted and can be completely avoided. Tobacco smoke has also been associated with a number of health problems including emphysema, bronchitis, lung cancer and so on. If a pregnant woman smokes, then it can lead to low birth weight in her child. If one is a smoker, he or she needs to seriously consider quitting. The decision for quitting needs to come from within, then an effective plan can be undertaken.

Most illegal drugs also act on the Central Nervous System. These drugs can depress the Central Nervous System, stimulate it, or alter and distort sensory responses. In all cases the net result is poor perception and decreased coping capabilities. Drug abuse also leads to psychological and/or physical dependence. Let us ask ourselves:

- Am I resorting to Alcohol, Smoking or Drugs to find answers to my problems?

- Is this the correct decision? **NO**

- How else can I solve my problems?

If alcohol or drug abuse are problems we need not let them get out of control and hamper our life. We need to seek professional help at the earliest possible time. We may want to contact a professional counselor, our family physician or a support organization like Alcoholics Anonymous (AA). The local address of Alcoholics Anonymous can be found in our telephone book.

Balanced Diet Plan for Stress Reduction and Healthful Living

The discussion in this chapter has been designed to help us understand the value and importance of maintaining a balanced diet, developing appropriate eating habits, and avoiding negative stress-coping practices like alcohol and drug abuse. Let us now sharpen our skills in developing and maintaining a diet plan with the help of Worksheet 7.2. Thoughts for Reflection 7.4 help us to ponder over some dietary goals which we need to implement in our daily life.

Thoughts for Reflection 7.4

Dietary Goals to Think About

- To avoid becoming overweight, consume only as much energy (calories) as is expended; if overweight, decrease energy intake and increase energy expenditure.

- Increase the consumption of complex carbohydrates and "naturally occurring" sugars from about 28 percent of energy intake to about 48 percent of energy intake.

- Reduce the consumption of refined and processed sugars by about 45 percent to supply about 10 percent of total energy intake.

- Total fat should be no more than 30.0% of the total calories. Reduce saturated-fat consumption to account for no more than 10 percent of total energy intake. Polyunsaturated fats should account for no more than 10.0% of energy intake, monounsaturated fats should make up the remainder (10.0-15.0%) of total calories.

- Reduce cholesterol consumption to no more than 300 mg per day.

- Limit the intake of sodium to 2400 milligrams (2.4 grams per day).

<u>Note</u>. From <u>Dietary Goals for the United States</u>, (2nd ed.) by Select Committee on Nutrition and Human Needs, 1986, Washington, D.C.: U.S. Senate Select Committee. Material under Public domain.

* * * * * * * * * * * * * * *

Worksheet 7.2
Ten-Step Balanced Diet Plan for
Stress Reduction and Healthful Living

Following are ten steps which will help us to plan our diet better for stress reduction and healthful living. Let us read the steps which follow and in the space provided write your own plan on how we would go about accomplishing that step.

Step 1. <u>Becoming aware of our dietary habits.</u>

Let us analyze our dietary habits. Skipping meals intensifies the stress response. The largest meal of the day needs to be taken earlier in the day. We need to be sure to find out whether we have three meals a day or not. Do we skip any meals? Which is our largest meal of the day?

_____

_____

_____

_____

_____

Step 2. <u>Establishing a balance among the six food groups.</u>

The United States Department of Agriculture's Food Pyramid suggests a balance of six food groups emphasizing bread and grains, vegetables and fruits, while placing less importance on meat, milk products, fats and sweets (Figure 7-1). Do we include food items from all the six food groups in appropriate quantities?

_____

_____

_____

_____

_____

Worksheet 7.2 Ten-Step Balanced Diet Plan for Stress Reduction and Healthful Living (Cont'd)

Step 3. <u>Planning to limit the intake of caffeinated beverages</u>

We have already seen that caffeine is a psuedostressor and causes a stress like response. Therefore, we should work to reduce our intake of caffeinated beverages. Some people like to stop them all at once, while others gradually taper their intake, and then substitute their intake with non caffeinated beverages. Let us write down and implement a strategy which suits us.

_____

_____

_____

_____

Step 4. <u>Planning to limit the daily intake of salt in our diet</u>

We have already seen that salt leads to retention of body water and may cause an increase in blood pressure. We need to avoid using any table salt and work at curbing our intake of "fast food" and "pre-cooked" food unless it is absolutely necessary. Let us work out a strategy to implement this plan.

_____

_____

_____

_____

Worksheet 7.2 Ten-Step Balanced Diet Plan for Stress Reduction and Healthful Living (Cont'd)

<u>**Step 5**</u>. <u>Planning to limit the daily intake of sugar</u>

Excessive sugar intake can paradoxically reduce the blood levels of sugar, causing hypoglycemia. This is due to the fact that temporarily high levels of sugar stimulate the release of insulin which causes blood sugar to fall (Smith, 1993). Therefore, limiting the intake of sugar helps in reducing stress.

_____

_____

_____

_____

<u>**Step 6**</u>. <u>Planning to stop smoking</u>

We have seen that smoking does not reduce stress. As discussed earlier, nicotine found in tobacco has an addictive effect on the stress response. To begin with record keeping of the number of cigarettes smoked, and seeking support from close friends is helpful. We need to then work at delaying the urge of smoking as many times as possible during the day. This can be achieved by diverting the mind to do something else at the time of the urge, and substituting the smoking habit with other constructive habits (like exercising). This way we can consistently work at cutting the number of cigarettes we smoke. Finally we need to decide upon a day and quit smoking completely. We need to religiously adhere to this commitment. Let us work out a definitive plan for ourselves to quit smoking.

_____

_____

_____

_____

Worksheet 7.2 Ten-Step Balanced Diet Plan for Stress Reduction and Healthful Living (Cont'd)

Step 7. Planning to avoid or reduce alcohol intake

Moderation with intake of alcohol and alcoholic beverages is vital in order to maintain balance and avoid stress. If we are not now practicing moderation, let us begin to work at establishing it.

_____

_____

_____

_____

Step 8. Supplementing vitamins and minerals in the diet

Establishing a balance in the daily intake of vitamins and minerals in the diet increases resistance to stress. It is best to choose a wide variety of foods to meet one's vitamin and mineral needs in place of supplementing items (See Table 7-3). Let us write out a plan to ensure that the needed vitamins and minerals are included in our diet.

_____

_____

_____

_____

Worksheet 7.2 Ten-Step Balanced Diet Plan for Stress Reduction and Healthful Living (Cont'd)

Step 9. Utilizing natural food products

Natural food products like yogurt have been suggested to help improve our stress-coping capabilities. One of the components of yogurt, Lactobacillus acidophilus has received attention. These bacteria are harmless and have been claimed to inhibit growth of pathogenic bacteria, boost the immune system, produce essential vitamins and enhance resistance to stress (Chaitow & Trenev, 1990; Lee, 1988; Schauss, 1990). Let us plan to increase consumption of natural food products in our diet.

_____

_____

_____

_____

_____

Step 10. Maintaining weight through regular monitoring and control

In order to reduce stress in our life, maintaining weight by weekly or bimonthly monitoring and working out an effective diet and exercise plan is vital. What is our plan?

_____

_____

_____

_____

* * * * * * * * * * * * * * *

Stress Management Principle # 7

**Enjoy balanced meals at regular times
and
cherish the gift!**

Summary Points

- Sleeping seven to eight hours daily, eating breakfast daily, consuming only planned snacks between meals, being at or near prescribed height adjusted weight, never smoking, moderate or no use of alcohol, and regular physical activity are some practices associated with good health.

- A healthy balanced diet when taken at regular times reduces stress and improves upon stress-coping capabilities.

- Maintaining weight based upon the ideal range for height, body frame, and gender is important for healthy living and stress reduction.

- Coffee, tea, or colas have <u>caffeine</u> which is a pseudostressor or a sympathomimetic agent, that is, it produces a stress like response in the body.

- Nicotine found in tobacco is also a sympathomimetic agent and produces stress.

- Alcohol and illegal drugs do <u>not</u> relieve stress but can only add to one's stress.

- Regulating salt and sugar intake in the diet is essential for managing stress.

- USRDA recommends no greater than 2400 mg of sodium per day in the diet.

- We need to observe moderation in consuming carbohydrates and proteins in our diet.

- Fats should be used only sparingly.

- Vitamins and minerals should be taken in recommended and optimum quantities.

- Water in the diet is the only constituent which should be taken in excess. It is recommended that we drink at least 8-10 glasses of water daily.

References and Further Readings

Belloc, N.B., & Breslow, L. (1972). Relationship of physical status and health practices. Preventive Medicine, 1, 409-421.

Chaitow, L. & Trenev, N. (1990). Probiotics. The revolutionary "friendly bacteria" way to vital health and well-being. Northamptonshire: Thorsons.

Cuthbertson, D. P. (1964). Physical injury and its effects on protein metabolism. In H. H. Munro and J. B. Allison (Eds.). Mammalian Protein Metabolism. Vol. II (pp. 374-414). New York, NY: Academic Press.

Girdano, D.E., Everly, G.S. Jr., Dusek, D.E. (1993). Controlling stress and tension. A holistic approach. Englewood Cliffs, N.J.: Prentice Hall.

Greenberg, J.S. (1993). Comprehensive stress management. (4th ed.). Dubuque, IA: William C. Brown Publishers.

Lee, W.H. (1988). The friendly bacteria. How lactobacilli and bifidobacteria can transform your health. New Canaan: Keats.

Schauss, A.G. (1990). Lactobacillus acidophilus: Method of action, clinical application and toxicity data. Journal of Advancement in Medicine, 3, 163-178.

Schlaadt, R.G. (1992). Alcohol use and abuse. Guilford, CT: The Dushkin Publishing Group.

Seventh Special Report to the U.S. Congress on Alcohol and Health. (1990, Jan.). Department of Health & Human Services, Public Health Service, Alcohol, Drug Abuse, and Mental Health Administration, National Institute on Alcohol Abuse and Alcoholism.

Smith, J.C. (1993). Understanding stress and coping. New York: Macmillan Publishing Company.

CHAPTER 8

REGULAR EXERCISE

Better to hunt in fields, for health unbought,
Than fee the doctor for a nauseous drought.
The wise, for cure, on exercise depend;
God never made his work, for man to mend.

John Dryden

Importance of Exercise

Exercise is not only good for physical health but also helps to enhance mental health. Improvement in both these dimensions contributes positively towards coping with stress more effectively. Exercise performed regularly promotes health by:

- providing higher energy levels

- improving body resistance to disease

- improving cardiovascular and respiratory fitness

- enhancing self-esteem and confidence

- regulating sleep patterns

- improving the ability to concentrate better

- increasing strength and stamina

- bringing about an overall positive and healthy outlook to life.

Various studies have supported the usefulness of regular exercise. Paffenberger and colleagues (1993) demonstrated that regular exercise during leisure time can protect people against premature deaths from any cause, particularly coronary heart disease. The exact mechanism by which exercise operates to reduce the incidence of coronary heart disease is debatable. A number of theories have been presented. Some researchers theorize that it is due to modification of feelings such as anger (Czajkowski, Hindelang, Dembroski, Mayerson, Parks, & Holland, 1990), while some attribute it to physiological reasons like increased blood flow to the brain or release of endorphins (Smith, 1993), and, finally, others believe it is due to diversion of attention from daily hassles and an accompanying relief in stress (Bahrke & Morgan, 1978). Whatever be the exact mechanism, there is enough positive evidence in support of regular exercise.

Types of Exercise

In order to describe types of exercise, a number of classifications are available. From a **biological** point of view, depending upon the oxygen utilization by the body, exercise can be classified into two types:

1.   Aerobic Exercise (from the word aerobic meaning "with oxygen") can be defined as exercise which does not require greater oxygen than can be taken by the body. Examples of aerobic activities include running, walking briskly, jogging, bicycling, swimming, rope jumping, and so on.

2.   Anaerobic Exercise (from the word anaerobic meaning "without oxygen") can be defined as exercise in which the body goes all out and the muscles rely heavily on production of energy without adequate oxygen. Examples of anaerobic activity would be sprinting 100 or 200 meters in which the body goes all out.

This above classification is more theoretical in its connotation. According to a **functional** point of view, exercise can be classified into the following types:

1.   Exercise for Circulatory and Respiratory Fitness. The circulatory system consists of the heart, blood, and blood vessels. The blood is an important carrier of oxygen to all cells of the body. This oxygen is utilized by the cells to produce necessary energy for daily activities. The respiratory system consists of airways and the lungs. The air which we breathe in is taken up by the lungs and oxygen is supplied to the blood. Therefore, both the circulatory and the respiratory systems are important in providing oxygen to produce necessary energy to the body. This plays an important role in managing stress. Examples of some activities which improve upon circulatory and respiratory fitness include brisk walking, jogging, running, aerobic dancing, and so on.

2.   Exercise for Enhancing Muscular Strength and Endurance. Muscular strength is the ability for achieving maximal performance. Muscular endurance is the ability to continuously work for a long period of time. Examples of some activities which improve upon muscular strength and endurance include pushups, situps, chinups, weight training, and so on.

3.   Exercise for Improving Body Flexibility. Flexibility is the ability of the body to perform various motions around the joints.   Examples of some activities include stretching, shoulder reach, trunk flexion, trunk extension, and so on.

4.   Exercise for Reducing Body Fat. Fat is normally deposited around the waist for men and on the thighs for women. Fat deposition also leads to atherosclerotic changes in arteries (narrowing with fatty deposition) and greater risk for coronary heart disease. Generally, exercise activities performed for circulatory, respiratory fitness, and muscular strength, described above, also help in burning off fat.

From an **operational** point of view, which is based upon the method of performance, exercise can be classified as follows:

1. Interval Training. This method includes exercising in bouts of hard activities separated by bouts of light exercise.

2. Continuous Training. This method includes exercising at a constant, rhythmic level of intensity for a long and uninterrupted period.

3. Circuit Training. This method includes completing a round of exercises known as "circuit." This "circuit" can be repeated for a desirable length of time and pace.

From an **applied practical** point of view, exercise can be classified as follows:

1. Competitive. This type of exercise includes performing for the purpose of competition, that is, in order to win an event. This competitive exercise produces great stress for many of us. One way to prevent this type of stress is to avoid competitive sports. If participation in competitive sports is inevitable, or one has a desire to do so, then one has to learn and develop appropriate coping skills in order to avoid potential negative consequences from stress.

2. Semi-Competitive. This type of exercise normally begins as a noncompetitive event, but when one gets into the mood, then one starts competing with others. This can also produce stress, and therefore, appropriate skills are required in coping.

3. Noncompetitive. These are activities which one performs purely for one's own health and satisfaction. There is no element of competition of any kind. This exercise does not produce any negative consequences associated with stress. On the other hand, noncompetitive exercise helps in counteracting the negative consequences of stress.

From the perspective of preventing, reducing, controlling and managing stress, any noncompetitive, aerobic exercise performed rhythmically, with regularity, is most beneficial. Examples of some activities which meet these criteria are described as follows:

• **Jogging/Running**. These activities are quite popular in the United States and very simple to perform. They require no special training and can be performed in almost any location and at any time of the day. All one needs is a good pair of running shoes. One also needs to have an empty stomach, that is, having not eaten anything for at least three to four hours. This activity can be performed individually or in groups. This is an excellent aerobic and rhythmic activity and is excellent for preventing, reducing, and managing stress.

• **Brisk Walking**. For older persons and people not used to exercising, this activity can be a very important initiating exercise. A walking technique needs to be natural and rhythmic. Use of correct posture and proper shoes are also important. This is a most inexpensive form of exercise, and if performed regularly, can yield rich dividends.

• **Cycling**. Cycling is also an aerobic rhythmic, cardio-respiratory exercise and is quite helpful in preventing, reducing, and managing stress. For this purpose cycling needs to be performed noncompetitively either outdoors or in a velodrome. For adequate results this activity needs to be done regularly for 30 minutes, at least three to four times a week.

• <u>**Swimming**</u>. This activity has often been called the most complete form of exercise. Swimming improves upon cardio-respiratory fitness, flexibility, muscular strength, and endurance. A significant advantage of swimming is that since the body is supported by water, risk of harm to joint and muscle is minimal. This activity is an effective means to prevent, reduce, and manage stress.

• <u>**Cross-Country Skiing**</u>. This activity also provides cardio-respiratory and muscular benefits. The whole body is utilized when performing this exercise. This activity is also helpful in preventing, reducing, and managing stress. It may appear that this activity can only be performed outdoors in the winter, but this is not so. One can also perform this activity indoors with the help of artificial equipment.

• <u>**Aerobic Dancing**</u>. This is an activity which has gained popularity over the past decade. This activity helps the whole body to obtain adequate cardio-respiratory fitness, flexibility, and muscular endurance. In this activity the mind is constantly engaged in achieving rhythmic coordination, and therefore, this helps divert attention from stress-producing thoughts.

• <u>**Activities Involving Use of Any Racquet**</u>. Activities such as racquet ball, tennis, table tennis, badminton, squash, and so on, if played non competitively, are helpful forms of exercise for improving upon cardio-respiratory fitness, flexibility, muscular strength, and endurance. These activities also relieve one from the potential harmful negative consequences of stress.

Before we proceed on to the steps towards initiating and sustaining an exercise program, let us become more aware of our exercise levels through completing Worksheet 8.1. Worksheet 8.2 helps us to determine target heart rates appropriate for us while performing exercise. Thoughts for Reflection 8.1 help us to become familiar with some principles for conditioning the body.

Worksheet 8.1
Enhancing Self-Awareness About Exercise Levels

Let us encircle the choice which best describes our behavior pertaining to exercise.

	Low	Moderate	High

		Low	Moderate		High	
1.	Level of physical activity at work	1	2	3	4	5
2.	Level of physical activity at leisure	1	2	3	4	5
3.	Regularity of exercise	1	2	3	4	5
4.	Number of times per week	1-2	3-4	5-6	>6
5.	Duration of exercise	<15 min	15-30/30-45 min	>45 min

6. Let us describe the type of exercise which we do?

_____

_____

_____

_____

_____

_____

_____

_____

_____

_____

_____

FEEDBACK ON WORKSHEET 8.1

From the point of view of preventing, reducing, controlling and managing stress, an exercise needs to be rhythmic, aerobic, noncompetitive, and performed for an adequate amount of time. This worksheet would have provided us with insight on our behavior pertaining to exercise. If our exercise levels are low, then we need to increase them. If our exercise levels are already high, then we need to sustain these efforts and attain regularity.

If the types of exercise we are performing are not holistic, that is, they do not contribute much to all the dimensions including cardio- respiratory fitness, flexibility, muscular strength, and endurance, then we need to choose such activities which contribute to all the dimensions. Some of such activities which have been described earlier include jogging/running, brisk walking, cycling, swimming, cross-country skiing, aerobic dancing, and activities involving the use of a racquet. We need to remember to include the components of rhythm, aerobics, and regularity in our exercise schedule.

* * * * * * * * * * * * * * * * *

Worksheet 8.2
Calculating Appropriate Target Heart Rate Range

In order for an exercise to produce optimum benefits for cardio-respiratory fitness and prevention of stress, exercise levels need to reach target heart rate for at least 15-30 minutes. In order to calculate our target heart rate range for exercising, proceed as follows:

1. We need to subtract our age from 220. Let us call this A.

    220 - Your Age = _____(A)

2. Let us take our pulse in a resting state for one minute. It is best to record one's pulse before getting up from bed in the morning to get a true resting heart rate. We have to feel the radial pulse at the wrist towards the side of the thumb (against the neck of the radius bone) or the carotid pulse in the neck against the Adam's Apple. We need to use our ring finger to feel the pulse so that there is no confusion with the pulse in the thumb, index, or middle fingers. Let us call this B and write it down in the space below.

    B = _____ beats / minute

3. Let us subtract B from A. Let us call this C.

    A - B = _____ -_____ = _____ (C)

4. Let us multiply C by 0.6. Let us call the result D.

    C x 0.6 = _____ x 0.6 = _____ (D)

5. Let us add B and D to obtain the <u>lower end</u> of our target heart rate range.

    B + D = _____ + _____ = _____

6. Let us multiply C by 0.8. Let us call the result E.

    C x 0.8 = _____ x 0.8 = _____ (E)

7. Let us add B and E to obtain the <u>upper end</u> of our target heart rate range.

    B + E = _____ + _____ = _____

FEEDBACK ON WORKSHEET 8.2

This worksheet would have provided us with an appropriate target heart rate range specific for our age. While exercising, it is extremely important to adhere to this target heart range and not exceed the upper limit at any time. This target heart range can be monitored while performing the exercise by taking one's own pulse. In case one is exceeding the target heart range, then one needs to slow down. Another "rough" method of estimating this is the "talk test." According to this test, if one is able to maintain normal conversation while exercising, then one is within the target heart range.

One needs to remain within the target heart range for 15-30 minutes in the conditioning phase of the exercise. Only after regular exercise for over six months to one year can this period be exceeded. We recommend that one does not exceed this period unless one wants to become a professional athlete.

It is also important to slowly and <u>not</u> suddenly achieve the target heart range. That is why it is recommended to initiate any exercise activity with <u>warming up and stretching</u>. It is also equally important to slowly and not suddenly turn back to the normal heart range after being in the target heart range for 15-30 minutes. Therefore, it is recommended to end any exercise activity with a slow <u>cool down</u>. This phenomenon acquires greater significance as we grow older.

* * * * * * * * * * * * * *

Thoughts for Reflection 8.1

Principles of Conditioning for Exercise

Conditioning the Mind

- Let us think about the benefits of an exercise program.

- We need to visualize what an exercise program can do for us.

- We have to find time for doing exercise. All of us can find sufficient time for exercise even if our schedules are extremely busy. Time availability needs to be created in the mind first.

- We can think of any friends or family members who can help us to monitor our regularity. We need to enter into an agreement with them.

- Let us be prepared to face a little discomfort in the form of aches and pains in the beginning when we initiate an exercise program.

Conditioning the Body

- Let us proceed to increase our exercise levels slowly. We need not initiate vigorous exercise suddenly. We have to build up the exercise levels slowly and gradually.

- We should remember to start an exercise program with warming up our body for at least 10 minutes. This includes activities performed at a slower pace.

- After the warming up phase we can go into the conditioning phase. We have to be careful not to overdo this phase. One of the criteria for judging the intensity is to find out our target heart rate (See Worksheet 8.2) and not exceed this phase for 15 -30 minutes.

- We have to always remember to cool down for 5 - 10 minutes after the intensive conditioning phase so that the heart rate comes back to near normal. Any easy paced activity will help to cool down after the strenuous conditioning phase.

- Maintaining regularity in exercising is vital for achieving maximum benefits.

Initiating and Sustaining an Exercise Program

We have discussed the importance, types of exercise, and enhanced our awareness regarding our exercise levels. We have also familiarized ourselves with the various principles required for conditioning the body and mind in order to prepare for exercise. Now we need to work towards initiating and sustaining regular exercise activities. Worksheet 8.3 has been designed to facilitate achieving this regularity. It is hoped that this Worksheet will foster insights into our behavior and help us adapt exercise lifestyles. Thoughts for Reflection 8.2 present us with some cautions which we need to keep in our mind before, during, and after exercise.

Worksheet 8.3
Five Steps toward Initiation and Sustenance of an Exercise Program

Following are five steps which will help us to initiate and sustain an exercise program. We have to read the text associated with each step. In the space provided let us write down our own plan as to how we would go about accomplishing that step.

Step 1. <u>Determining our exercise levels.</u>

An awareness about our exercise levels is the first step toward developing our own plan of improvement. Based upon feedback from Worksheet 8.1 in the space provided below, let us rate our exercise levels and write down what, how, and how much we need to improve.

_____

_____

_____

_____

Step 2. <u>Checking before exercise.</u>

Before proceeding to initiate an exercise program, let us respond to the following questions. If we answer yes or are not sure about any of the questions below, we need to consult our physician before beginning an exercise program.

* Is there a history of any heart disease in my family?

    _____ yes   _____ no   _____ not sure

* Have I ever been diagnosed to have any heart disease?

    _____ yes   _____ no   _____ not sure

* Have I ever suffered from chest pains?

    _____ yes   _____ no   _____ not sure

Worksheet 8.3 Five Steps toward Initiation and Sustenance of an Exercise Program (Cont'd)

- Do I have shortness of breath while climbing up a flight of stairs?

    _____ yes   _____ no   _____ not sure

- Have I ever been diagnosed to have diabetes mellitus or detected for high blood sugar or sugar in urine or have complaints of excessive hunger, thirst, or increased urination?

    _____ yes   _____ no   _____ not sure

- Am I a smoker?

    _____ yes   _____ no   _____ not sure

- Am I over 35 years of age and have not exercised regularly?

    _____ yes   _____ no   _____ not sure

- Have I ever been diagnosed to have high total serum cholesterol levels (particularly LDL or "bad cholesterol")?

    _____ yes   _____ no   _____ not sure

- Am I taking any prescribed medication(s)?

    _____ yes   _____ no   _____ not sure

- Do I have any other medical problem(s) / disability(ies)?

    _____ yes   _____ no   _____ not sure

Step 3. Starting an exercise program

Having decided that we want to initiate an exercise program, let us choose an appropriate place. Let us practice exercise either early in the morning when our stomach is empty or late afternoon before dinner. It is important to remember that exercise habits need to be changed gradually. We should increase duration by one to five minutes every other session.

Worksheet 8.3 Five Steps toward Initiation and Sustenance of an Exercise Program (Cont'd)

An exercise program always has three parts: <u>warm-up,</u> <u>conditioning,</u> and <u>cool down</u>.   Let us practice all three stages meticulously. Let us now make a plan to start our exercise program if we do not already have one.

_____

_____

_____

_____

_____

_____

<u>Step 4</u>. <u>Braving the initial "teething" problems</u>

It is usual to have pain, discomfort and tiredness in the initial few days of starting our exercise plan. Let us be prepared for these and write down in the space below all the anticipated problems we are likely to face and how we are going to manage them. This will help us adapt to change in our exercise plan.

_____

_____

_____

_____

_____

_____

_____

Worksheet 8.3 Five Steps toward Initiation and Sustenance of an Exercise Program (Cont'd)

Step 5. <u>Sustaining regularity in exercise</u>

Just like the plant in the pot withers away without regular replenishment by water, any good habit, if not incorporated into a regular plan, does not provide us with complete benefits. Now we have to make a plan for ourselves as to how we would like to sustain our exercise program.

_____

_____

_____

_____

_____

_____

_____

* * * * * * * * * * * * * * *

Thoughts for Reflection 8.2

Cautions with Exercise

- We should not start vigorous exercise suddenly. We have to make a plan before we implement it.

- We have to be careful not to overexert. Common signs of overexertion are:
    - frequent headaches
    - breathing difficulties and shortness of breath
    - excessive tiredness and fatigue which lasts over a longer period of time
    - nausea or vomiting after exercise
    - severe pain all over the body especially in overworked muscles
    - inability to perform daily activities
    - excessive strain of any part of the body

- We have to be aware of abnormal signs when exercising. Common abnormal signs are:
    - chest pain
    - dizziness, fainting
    - fits
    - irregular heart movements as felt by irregular palpitations
    - sustained pain in the joints
    - swelling in any part of the body after exercise

- We have to drink plenty of water and fluids with electrolytes to avoid getting dehydrated.

- We should not exercise when our stomach is full. We have to wait for at least 2 hours for exercise if we have eaten something.

- During pregnancy, the expectant mother should consult her physician before following a regular exercise schedule.

- We need to wear comfortable outfit and do not wear very tight clothes. Our shoes need to be selected carefully and not cause us blisters, corns and sores.

* * * * * * * * * * * * * * *

Stress Management Principle # 8

**Let us start an exercise program
and
keep exercising regularly.**

Summary Points

- Regular exercise promotes health by providing higher energy levels, improving body resistance to disease, enhancing self-esteem and confidence, increasing strength and stamina, and bringing about an overall positive and healthy outlook to life.

- Regular exercise helps to prevent, reduce, control, and manage stress.

- Biologically, exercise can be classified as aerobic and anaerobic.

- Functionally, exercise can be classified as activities improving cardio-respiratory fitness, activities enhancing muscular strength and endurance, activities improving body flexibility, and activities reducing fat.

- Operationally, exercise can be classified as interval, continuous, and circuit training.

- Practically, exercise can be classified as competitive, semi-competitive, and non-competitive.

- In order for exercise to produce optimum benefits for cardio-respiratory fitness, prevention, reduction, and management of stress, the exercise levels need to reach target heart rate for at least 15-30 minutes.

- Conditioning the body and mind are prerequisites for initiating and sustaining any exercise program.

- Steps of an ideal exercise program include **warm-up** (10 minutes), **conditioning** (maintaining the target heart rate for 15-30 minutes), and **cool down** (10 minutes).

- Regularity in exercising is extremely important in order to obtain maximum benefits.

References and Further Readings

Bahrke, M.S., & Morgan, W.P. (1978). Anxiety reduction following exercise and meditation. Cognitive Therapy and Research, 2, 323-333.

Czajkowski, S.M., Hindelang, R.D., Dembroski, T.M., Mayerson, S.E., Parks, E.B., Holland, J.C. (1990). Aerobic fitness, psychological characteristics and cardiovascular reactivity to stress. Health psychology, 9, 676-692.

Girdano, D.E., Everly, G.S. Jr., Dusek, D.E. (1993). Controlling stress and tension. A holistic approach. Englewood Cliffs, N.J.: Prentice Hall.

Greenberg, J.S. (1993). Comprehensive stress management. (4th ed.). Dubuque, IA: William C. Brown Publishers.

Paffenberger, R.S. Jr., Hyde, R.T., Wing, A.L., Lee, I.M., Jung,D.L., & Kampert, J.B. (1993). The association of changes in physical activity level and other life style characteristics with mortality among men. The New England Journal of Medicine, 328, 538-545.

Smith, J.C. (1993). Understanding stress and coping. New York: Macmillan Publishing Company.

CHAPTER 9

EFFICIENT TIME MANAGEMENT

To Daffodils

Fair daffodils, we weep to see
You haste away so soon:
As yet the early-rising sun
Has not attain'd his noon.
Stay, stay,
Until the hasting day
Has run
But to the even-song;
And, having pray'd together, we
Will go with you along.
We have short time to stay, as you,
We have as short a spring;
As quick a growth to meet decay,
As you or anything.

Robert Herrick

Importance of Time Management

Time is one of our most precious resources. All of us have the same time available to us, and this time is limited. Our existence on Earth has a limited time frame. We are not even aware how much time is available in our life. Therefore, we need to make the best use of whatever time is available to us. Moreover, the way we utilize this time determines success in accomplishing our desired goals. In present times this success is an important determinant of our happiness and peace of mind. If we utilize our time judiciously and efficiently, we can become more successful. On the contrary, if we are unable to utilize our time appropriately, our productivity is decreased. This inefficiency in managing our time may create problems. It leads to unfulfillment of our expectations and desired goals, which in turn can become a great source of stress for us. Therefore, management of time efficiently and effectively acquires great significance.

Another important dimension with regard to utilization of our time is to have appropriate **balance** in our activities. We need to allocate adequate time for physical activities, mental enrichment, social interactions, and spiritual well being. All these dimensions are important spokes of a "holistic wheel" for harmony in life as shown in Figure 9-1.

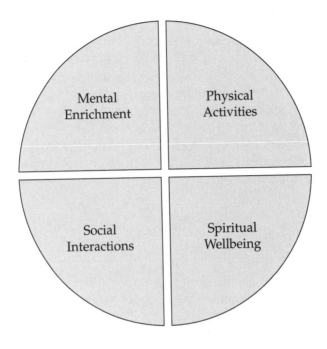

Figure 9-1 "Holistic Wheel" of Harmony in Life

One popular management principle, in the context of time management, is the <u>Pareto Principle</u>. According to this principle, most of the desired key results are obtained by only a few of our total activities. On the other hand, the majority of other activities generate only a few of the key results. Pareto estimated that this relationship was 20 percent to 80 percent in most situations, that is, 80 percent of the results would be derived from 20 percent of the objectives, while 80 percent of the objectives would yield only 20 percent of the results. Therefore, **priority** of effort may be given to those objectives identified as **"the critical few"** (Liebler, Levine, & Rothman, 1992). This approach of learning and practicing to prioritize our daily activities and tasks, in order to optimize results, will be the basis for our discussion on efficient time management.

Manifestations of Poor Time Management

Poor time management seems to be a "universal" problem. It is generally shown from studies on time management that the majority of us, for most of the time, admit to not managing our time very well and acknowledge that this does create stress in our lives. Some of the manifestations of poor time management are as follows:

- Unfulfilled expectations

- Inability to be on time for appointments

- Hurrying to be on time

- Poor planning

- Inability to achieve desired objectives

- Tiredness and fatigue due to unplanned down time

- Regret over missed deadlines

- Disappointments

- Inadequate time for rest

- Borrowing time from timeslots for family, work, leisure, free time, or personal relationships

- Constant feeling of being overwhelmed

- Feeling of "too much going on"

- Worrying about how to get things done

- Inability to deliver goods on time

- Insecure feelings about the future

- Regrets about the past

Therefore, poor time management is an important source of stress and leads to negative harmful consequences. These undue negative consequences are self inflicted and can be easily prevented if we understand, apply, and follow the basic principles of time management.

Self understanding is a prerequisite to making any change, particularly in changing our behavior in relation to efficient time management (Januz & Jones, 1981). Therefore, before we proceed to learn about the basic principles of efficient time management, we need to gain an insight into our own behavior and find out whether managing time is a problem for us. This understanding will provide us with a benchmark as to where we start our efforts at managing time efficiently and effectively. Worksheet 9.1 has been designed to help us enhance this understanding. Thoughts for Reflection 9.1 helps us to ponder about some of the barriers which may be preventing us from managing our time efficiently.

Worksheet 9.1
Enhancing Awareness On How We Spend Our Time

Let us sit down, relax, and respond to the following questions honestly. There are no right or wrong answers. This worksheet will enhance our own awareness about how we are using our time.

1. In the past week, was I late for any appointment(s)?

    ___ yes   ___ no   ___ not sure

    If yes, how many times? ___ out of ___ times.

    Reasons:

    _____

    _____

    _____

2. In the past week, did I miss my breakfast, lunch, or supper in order to be on time for some task?

    ___ yes   ___ no   ___ not sure

    If yes, how many times? ___ out of 21 times.

    Reasons:

    _____

    _____

3. Do I feel lethargic or tired often?

    ___ yes   ___ no   ___ not sure

    If yes, what do you think causes this to happen?

    _____

    _____

Worksheet 9.1 Enhancing Awareness on How We Spend Our Time (Cont'd)

4. In the past week, did I miss any deadline at work or any other personal obligation?

    ___ yes   ___ no   ___ not sure

    If yes, when?

    _____

    _____

    Reasons:

    _____

    _____

    _____

5. Am I content with the amount of time which I am devoting towards rest and sleep?

    ___ yes   ___ no   ___ not sure

    Reasons:

    _____

    _____

    _____

    _____

6. In the past week, did I ever feel that "too much was going on" in my life?

    ___ yes   ___ no   ___ not sure

    If yes, when?

    _____

    _____

    Reasons:

    _____

    _____

    _____

Worksheet 9.1 Enhancing Awareness on How We Spend Our Time (Cont'd)

7. How much time do I give for:

Category	Too much	Enough	Not Adequate
• Work			
• Family			
• Personal Relationships/ Friends			
• Exercise			
• Your Own Free Time			
• Leisure and Recreation			

8. Do I consider myself being overwhelmed at the present moment in my life?

___ yes   ___ no   ___ not sure

Reasons:

_____

_____

_____

_____

_____

_____

Worksheet 9.1 Enhancing Awareness on How We Spend Our Time (Cont'd)

9. In the past week, was I able to accomplish all my duties satisfactorily and in a timely manner?

 ___ yes   ___ no   ___ not sure

Reasons:

_____

_____

_____

10. Do I manage my time well?

 ___ yes   ___ no   ___ not sure

Reasons:

_____

_____

_____

FEEDBACK ON WORKSHEET 9.1

Now that we have completed Worksheet 9.1 we have acquired an awareness on how we are spending our time. If time management appears to be a problem for us, we will have to strive hard to work at managing our time more efficiently. This chapter will provide us with some ideas for managing our time more efficiently. These ideas can only serve as possible guidelines. The ultimate decision and actions to be taken have to come from within us. Only we can make a difference as to how efficiently we will manage our time.

* * * * * * * * * * * * * *

Thoughts for Reflection 9.1

Barriers to Efficient Time Management

- **Inability to prioritize**. If we are not familiar with the basic principles of prioritization, or do not have the necessary skills, or are not willing to prioritize, then any of these situations will act as a barrier to efficient time management. Prioritizing daily activities, short-term objectives, and long-term goals are central to efficient time management.

- **Inability to say "no."** It is simply not possible to please everyone sometimes. Nor is it possible to please some people all the time. Therefore, the ability to say "no" to others, if we want to say "no," even if it may be somewhat displeasing, is an important practice in efficiently managing our time. This allows us to accomplish our goals and objectives and not become distracted.

- **Imbalance in life**. We may be neglecting or overindulging in some of our daily activities. We may be overactive physically while neglecting our mental enrichment. Or we may be socially very active but have low levels of physical activity. Or we may be completely "bankrupt" spiritually. Or we may be involved in too many mental activities so much so that we become isolated socially. We need balance in life.

- **Too many improperly planned desires**. The mind is a very powerful source of generating desires. There is nothing wrong with having desires per se, but if we do not have a proper plan to accomplish these desires, then they do more harm than good. We need to select a few key desires, make a plan to achieve them, and work at the plan.

- **Lack of focus**: If we are not focused on our goals, we will most often spend our time on misdirected activities. We need to think and decide what we want to achieve and then make focused efforts in order to optimize the use of our time.

- **Procrastination**: The habit of delaying accomplishments of any task to the very last minute is an important barrier in effective time management. Once we know what we need to do, we need to accomplish it as soon as possible.

* * * * * * * * * * * * * *

Approaches to Time Management

Time management has acquired greater significance in modern times. Never before in history has time management been given such importance. Present life has become much more fast paced compared to the past. Therefore, approaches for time management need to address present times. There are a plethora of ideas which have been suggested for time management (Assagioli, 1973; Davis, Eshelman, & McKay, 1988; Eliot & Breo, 1989; Greenberg, 1993; Greenwald, 1973; Lakein, 1973; Levinson, 1990; Mackenzie, 1972; Smith 1993; Swindoll, 1982). In essence, all these approaches to time management emphasize the need to **prioritize** our daily activities and implement a plan to achieve them. From a practical point of view, the basic technique consists of the following components:

- Developing awareness about how one spends one's time.

- Setting long-term goals.

- Identifying short-term objectives to accomplish these goals.

- Establishing priorities.

- Concrete decision-making about key priorities.

- Realistic scheduling and elimination of low priorities.

- Overcoming possible barriers.

- Implementing the plan of priorities to manage time efficiently.

This basic technique of time management helps us in achieving our long term goals, as well as assists us in accomplishing our daily activities. Developing a longer time horizon is important from a future perspective, while accomplishment of daily activities is important from a present perspective. Both these dimensions play an important role in preventing and reducing undue stress in our life. In this chapter we shall be focusing primarily on managing time with respect to accomplishing daily activities and tasks. The skills pertaining to setting goals and objectives have been elaborated on in Chapter 10. Therefore, in this chapter we shall not discuss what goals to set and how to define objectives in meeting those goals. We assume that goals have already been set, and from there we will elaborate on a practical technique for managing time for accomplishing daily activities and tasks. Let us now complete Worksheet 9.2 which has been designed for this purpose. We also need to ponder on Thoughts for Reflection 9.2 which helps us appreciate the importance of having time for ourselves and focusing on the present. Thoughts for Reflection 9.3 provides us with some ideas on how we can save time.

Thoughts for Reflection 9.2

It Has Been Quite Some Time . . .

It has been quite some time since I have noticed nature and its beauty around me. When was the last time I looked and pondered on the blue, beautiful, magnanimous sky, the majestic snow-peaked tall mountains, the green thick forests, the bright shining sun, or other beauties of nature.

It has been even longer since I reflected on the daily intricate and seemingly small events around me. When was the last time I noticed a child's smile, a gesture of kindness by people around me, a token of appreciation, or other gifts of human love.

Rather, I have been too busy with daily hassles — in meeting deadlines, fulfilling obligations, yielding to demands, and chasing desires. I have been either regretting past events or worrying about future happenings.

- Am I doing the right thing?

- Am I utilizing my time wisely?

- Am I happy, contented, and satisfied?

- Do I have peace of mind?

Two issues seem apparent. First, I have not taken enough time for myself. Second, I have ignored the most important frontier, "the now!" I have not completely understood the true value of "today" and the importance of having time available for myself. I need to reflect and restore the inherent joy of having time for myself now.

* * * * * * * * * * * * * *

Worksheet 9.2
Practical Steps to Time Management

We need to seek out a quiet place and complete the following worksheet. We can photocopy this worksheet if we require more space.

Step 1.   Developing awareness about how we are currently spending our time.

Worksheet 9.1 has already provided us with some insights. Now we can summarize those findings in a chronological and meaningful sequence in the space provided below:

Past one week:

Activities Desired	Activities Performed

Past one month:

Activities Desired	Activities Performed

Worksheet 9.2 Practical Steps to Time Management (Cont'd)

Past one year:

Activities Desired	Activities Performed

A comparison between the activities desired and performed will provide us with an understanding of the gap which exists and needs to be rectified.

Step 2. List of All Desired Activities.

Let us now make a comprehensive list of all the activities which we need to accomplish in a chronological manner.

Today:

_____

_____

_____

_____

_____

_____

_____

Worksheet 9.2 Practical Steps to Time Management (Cont'd)

<u>Within the next week:</u>

_____

_____

_____

_____

_____

_____

<u>Within the next month:</u>

_____

_____

_____

_____

_____

_____

<u>Within the next year:</u>

_____

_____

_____

_____

_____

_____

Worksheet 9.2 Practical Steps to Time Management (Cont'd)

<u>Step 3</u>. <u>Establishing Priorities</u>.

Now we have to ask ourselves, "What is the best use of my time right now?" Having reflected upon this question we need to classify all desired activities into three categories: A = high value (activities which need to be done absolutely and immediately), B = medium value (activities which need to be accomplished as soon as possible), C = low value (activities which need to be done at some time or may be even ignored).

	Category A	Category B	Category C
<u>Today:</u>			
<u>Within the next week:</u>			
<u>Within the next month:</u>			
<u>Within the next year:</u>			

Worksheet 9.2 Practical Steps to Time Management (Cont'd)

<u>Step 4</u>. <u>Reassessing priorities</u>.

Everyday before going to bed, we need to reassess the priorities set in Step 3 and see which ones remain unfulfilled. We need to identify any obstacles or barriers which may have been responsible. Then we need to make necessary changes. In the space provided below we can record our observations.

_____

_____

_____

_____

_____

_____

_____

_____

FEEDBACK ON WORKSHEET 9.2

This worksheet would have helped us prioritize our daily activities as well as possible activities in the near future. We need to make focused efforts at achieving activities listed in Category A. After having accomplished the activities in Category A, we need to proceed to complete those activities listed in Category B. Only after accomplishing tasks in these activities do we look at tasks in Category C, even though they may appear to be simple and easy. We should not be allured by this simplicity and only focus on the importance of the activities.

* * * * * * * * * * * * * *

Thoughts for Reflection 9.3

Ways We Can Save Time

- Establishing priorities.

- Adhering to established priorities.

- Avoiding procrastination.

- Avoiding gossip.

- Having a balance in types of activities.

- Avoiding unnecessary socialization.

- Self-organization.

- Delegating tasks.

- Not seeking perfection always.

- Having faith in the ability of others.

- Overcoming undue frustration.

- Simplifying the tasks.

- Refusing when we would like to refuse.

- Having free time to reflect and plan.

- Thinking before doing.

- Not overindulging in only pleasure seeking activities.

- Making written lists of daily tasks to be done.

* * * * * * * * * * * * * *

Stress Management Principle # 9

"Do it Now!"

Summary Points

- Time is a precious resource which needs to be managed efficiently and effectively.

- We need to have appropriate balance in our physical activities, mental enrichment, social interactions, and spiritual well being.

- According to Pareto's Principle most of the desired key results are obtained by only a few of our activities, while the majority of our activities generate only a few key results. Usually this ratio is 80: 20.

- Some manifestations of poor time management include unfulfilled expectations, inability to be on time for appointment, hurrying, disappointment, regrets, and so on.

- Self-understanding is a prerequisite to efficient time management.

- Barriers to efficient time management include inability to prioritize, inability to say "no," imbalance in life, too many improperly planned desires, lack of focus, and procrastination.

- Central to all approaches to time management is the understanding and practice of the skill to prioritize.

- There are two important things for peace and happiness: having time for oneself and focusing on the present.

References and Further Readings

Assagioli, R. (1973). <u>The act of will</u>. New York: The Viking Press.

Burke, C.R., Hall, D.R., & Hawley, D. (1986). Living with stress. Clackamas, OR: Wellsource Inc.

Davis, M., Eshelman, E.R., & McKay, M. (1988). <u>The relaxation and stress reduction workbook</u> (3rd ed.). Oakland, CA: New Harbinger Publications.

Eliot, R.S., & Breo, D. L. (1989). <u>Is it worth dying for? How to make stress work for you-not against you</u> (rev. ed.) (p. 216). New York, NY: Bantam Books.

Greenberg, J.S. (1993). <u>Comprehensive stress management</u> (4th ed.). Dubuque,IA: William C. Brown Publishers.

Greenwald, H. (1973). <u>Direct decision therapy</u>. San Diego, CA: EDITS.

Hanson, P. G. (1986). <u>The joy of stress</u>. New York, NY: Andrews and McNeal.

Januz, L.R., & Jones, S.K. (1981). <u>Time management for executives</u>. New York, NY: Charles Scribner's Sons.

Lakein, A. (1973). <u>How to get control of your time and your life</u>. New York: Signet.

Levinson, J.C. (1990). <u>The ninety-minute hour</u>. New York, NY: E. P. Dutton.

Liebler, J.G., Levine, R.E., & Rothman, J. (1992). <u>Management principles for health professionals</u> (2nd ed.). Gaithersburg, MD: Aspen Publishers Inc.

Mackenzie, A. (1972). <u>The time trap</u>. New York, NY: AMACOM.

Rice, P. L. (1992). <u>Stress and health</u> (2nd ed.). Pacific Grove, CA: Brooks/Cole Publishing Company.

Smith, J. C. (1993). <u>Creative stress management. The 1-2-3 cope system</u>. Englewood Cliffs, NJ: Prentice Hall, Inc.

Swindoll, C.R. (1982). <u>Strengthening your grip: How to live confidently in an aimless world</u>. Dallas, TX: Word Publishing.

CHAPTER 10

IMPLEMENTING A STRESS REDUCTION PLAN

Rabbi ben Ezra

Grow old along with me!
The best is yet to be,
The last of life, for which the first was made:
Our times are in his hand
Who saith, 'A whole I planned
Youth shows but half; trust God: see all, nor be
afraid!'

Robert Browning

Importance of Implementing a Plan

Any intention — however noble it may be, any plan — however well conceived it may be, any desire — however chaste it may be, **unless implemented,** cannot produce the necessary results. We need to implement our intentions, plans, and desires in order to obtain the necessary results. The purpose of this workbook has been to provide us with practical suggestions toward preventing, reducing, and managing the harmful negative consequences of stress in our daily lives and enable us to effectively manage changes which are an inevitable part of our life. These practical suggestions, if not implemented in our lives, will be meaningless. We need to make conscious efforts at integrating these suggestions in our daily activities. This will foster positive health and promote our well-being.

The starting point in the process of implementation is to take stock of whatever resources are available to us. In implementing a stress reduction plan, a prerequisite is to have **self-motivation.** Unless and until we are motivated at bringing about change in our life, nobody can force us to make that change. We need to be committed. We need to have faith in ourselves and the techniques which we are going to implement. We also need to be aware of what needs to be changed.

Another prerequisite for success is the **degree of changeability** in what it is that we intend to change in our behavior. This changeability varies from individual to individual and is person specific. For example, applying relaxation techniques may be more changeable for some of us while difficult for others who have a more rigid lifestyle, or applying anxiety-coping techniques may be more changeable for some of us while others may find it more difficult, and so on. From a practical point of view, we need to prioritize and put forth our efforts into those behavior patterns which are **changeable** and **important** (Green & Kreuter, 1991). We need to identify for ourselves, on our own, which behaviors are less changeable and which behaviors are more changeable for us and which behaviors are more important and which activities are less important for us. The behaviors which are more important and more changeable need our first priority. Then we need to alter behaviors which are more important but less changeable. After accomplishing these two sets of behaviors, we can tackle behaviors which are less important and more changeable. Behaviors which are less important and less changeable need to be ignored. This aspect will be presented in Worksheet 10.2 later on in this Chapter.

After having this requisite motivation and conditioning, we need to identify which friends, co-workers, family members, associates, and so on, can help us in our efforts at implementing our stress reduction plan. We need to take them into confidence and share our plan. We need to solicit their support in helping us adhere to the plan. They will provide us with necessary mental, emotional, and social support which will help us not to deviate from our decisions. We also need to procure any special accessory or equipment required for implementing the desired set of behaviors. For example, for initiating a cross country skiing exercise program, we need to have ski gear, appropriate clothing, conditioning, and location.

We also need to make definitive time allocations for implementing our plan. This will entail scheduling the activities for desired behaviors (as suggested in several worksheets throughout each chapter of this workbook) into our daily plan however busy we may apparently be. We need to allocate regular "blocks of time" for implementing techniques for prevention, reduction, and management of stress.

Finally, we need to make this stress reduction plan fit into our overall scheme of life. This implies that we have clarity about where we want to be, or in other words — what is our goal? We also need to have clarity as to how we will achieve this goal, that is, which objectives will lead us to that goal.

Determining Goals, Objectives, and Targets

Goal Setting

Goals are the sum total of projections of our long-term plans. Goals are an indication of what we want to accomplish in our life. Goals signify a mission, an ambition, a purpose, and overall aim in life. These goals are oftentimes broad in nature. We need to identify goals for ourselves in different spheres of life, namely **personal, professional, social, and spiritual**. An example of a personal goal would be achieving personal happiness and peace of mind; an example of a professional goal could be achieving a certain position within an organization; an example of a social goal could be marital contentment; and an example of a spiritual goal could be achieving world peace. Attaining goals within all these spheres is important from the perspective of deriving balance, harmony, and satisfaction in life. If any of these components is missing, then life will not be holistic and complete happiness will elude us. A person without goals is also likely to have greater stress in life because of undirected, aimless efforts.

"Goal analysis" or "goal setting" is a procedure useful in helping us describe the meaning of what we want to achieve in terms of attitude and understanding (Mager, 1972). The concept of setting goals implies that it is not necessarily important to achieve things in the "right way" but to do the "right things." An understanding of what these "right things" are for us is central to goal setting. The sense of direction in our activities is essentially an internally driven behavior. A number of theories have been presented to explain this behavior. One of the most popular theories in psychology, Maslow's **Hierarchy of Needs Theory** on Motivation (Maslow, 1954, 1962) identifies the following five levels of needs:

(1) physiological (food, clothing, shelter, sex, and so on)

(2) security and safety (protection from physical and emotional harm)

(3) love, affection, belonging, and social acceptance

(4) self-esteem (internal factors like self-respect, autonomy, achievement and external factors such as status, recognition, attention, and so on)

(5) self-actualization (to achieve one's maximum potential)

According to Maslow a person progresses from lower level needs, such as physiological, security and safety, to higher level needs, such as self-esteem and self-actualization, during the course of one's lifetime. He hypothesized that the ultimate goal in life for all human beings was to reach self-actualization. According to this theory it was important to accomplish a lower level of need before proceeding to the next level.

However, later research led to a modification of this theory. Clayton Alderfer (1969) revised this concept and presented an **ERG Theory**. ERG is an acronym of the words Existence, Relatedness, and Growth. These are the three groups of core needs. Existence is concerned with basic material requirements (same as Maslow's physiological and safety needs), Relatedness is similar to Maslow's love need and the external component of Maslow's self-esteem classification, and Growth is similar to the internal self-esteem component and self-actualization of Maslow's theory. However, the key features which differentiate this ERG theory with Maslow's theory are as follows: (1) more than one level of need may be operative at the same time, and (2) if gratification of a higher level need is blocked, then the desire to satisfy a lower level need is increased. This ERG theory has greater scientific validation (Robbins, 1989).

This basic understanding in motivation is important in enabling us to set our goals. We need to be conscious about the "level of need" operating within our mind at any time. We also need to understand that the ultimate goal in life is to achieve our maximum potential or self-actualization.

Establishing Objectives.

Objectives can be defined as concerted, directed, focused stepwise efforts at achieving goals. Objectives are more precise in comparison to goals and represent smaller steps. Some of the attributes in establishing objectives are as follows:

- precision (clear and not vague statements directed toward goal accomplishment)

- determined time frame (for example, one month, one year)

- realistic (accomplishable within available time frame and resources)

- sequenced (logical flow of steps is helpful in reaching the goal)

- preferably written (writing out objectives enhances clarity and provides a documented record for future reference)

- proactive (use of action verbs and self-driven)

- measurable (changes need to be monitored in concrete terms)

- behaviorally oriented (implying specific behavior changes which need to be accomplished)

<u>Example of an objective</u>:

"I will be able to identify one <u>irrational belief</u> responsible for causing my work-related anxiety, <u>within the next one week</u>, and achieve proficiency in practicing <u>progressive muscle relaxation</u> (PMR), as evinced by a feeling of relaxation by my body, after ten minutes of daily practice, performed after coming home from work."

This objective may appear to be slightly verbose, but we have attempted to explain most of the attributes within this example. While formulating objectives for ourselves, only we can be the best judge as to which criteria need inclusion and which criteria can be excluded.

Deciding Targets

In order to achieve practical accomplishment of goals and objective, we need to perform a number of day-to-day activities. Identifying these day-to-day activities in advance is important in planning. This process is known as deciding targets. An example of a target would be: "I will, at 6:00pm, after returning from work, perform progressive muscle relaxation."

Let us now, with the help of Worksheet 10.1 set our goals and establish objectives. Worksheet 10.2 has been designed to prioritize our objectives. Worksheet 10.3 will help us to decide upon daily targets in order to accomplish prioritized objectives. We can use the format presented in Worksheet 10.3 for deciding daily targets for different objectives from either photocopies of the worksheet or a separate blank sheet of paper.

Thoughts for Reflection 10.1 will help us to ponder some aspects to keep in mind before setting goals and establishing objectives. Thoughts for Reflection 10.2 present some Eastern thoughts on obtaining results.

Thoughts for Reflection 10.1

Points to Ponder

Goal Setting and Establishing Objectives . . .

. . .   are not wishful thinking or daydreaming.

. . .   are positive, and proactive.

. . .   are an individual activity which no one else can do
          for us.

. . .   are not something to regret about the past or worry
          about the future.

. . .   are a powerful tool for success in life.

. . .   are an act of discipline.

. . .   are effective for reducing stress, managing change, and
          promoting health.

* * * * * * * * * * * * * *

Thoughts For Reflection 10.2

Eastern Views on Obtaining Results

Most of our stress is due to expectations of obtaining results arising from our actions. We are not sure what results we will get and this is often a source of fear, anxiety and other forms of stress. According to Eastern philosophy the results are bound to follow any action. This is the basic law of nature: the law of "cause and effect." The uncertain nature of results is also mandatory. According to this theory results are dependent on the following three aspects:

- <u>Effort</u>: No result can occur without an **effort** on our part. **Effort** is the first and foremost step towards obtaining results.

- <u>Direction</u>: If our **effort** lacks an appropriate direction, then we shall not be able to obtain the necessary results. Therefore, having a **direction** or focus is important to achieving success in our **effort**.

- <u>Unknown factor</u>: Even after applying an **effort** in an appropriate **direction**, success sometimes does not come. This is due to the "unknown factor" which is operating in the "universal system of law." Religious-minded people refer to this as "God," Scientists attribute this to "Probability" and "Chance." Without being unduly concerned about the semantics, the basic fact remains that we need to acknowledge and accept this inherent phenomenon. We need to then strengthen our mind and not be perturbed if the results do not go our way.

The only aspects over which we have control are **effort** and **direction**. Having applied our **effort** and that **effort** in the right **direction**, we need to think no further. We need to develop an attitude of bearing whatever the results may be. If they are good, we need to be thankful to the "Unknown;" if they are not to our expectation, we need to think what went wrong, how we can rectify anything, if at all and accept the result with fortitude and grace. If the result has been negative, we also need to rethink about changing our **effort** and **direction**, that is, the behavior, if it is faulty.

* * * * * * * * * * * * * *

Worksheet 10.1
Determining Goals and Objectives

Let us seek out a quiet place and complete this worksheet. We need to write out an optimum number of goals and objectives, that is, not to have too few or too many. <u>It is also important to write these out</u>. We need to periodically reexamine, reassess, and redefine our goals and objectives. We could make photocopies of this basic format or work on a separate sheet of paper.

Day & Date: _____

A. <u>Setting Goals</u>.

Personal Goal:

_____

_____

_____

Professional Goal:

_____

_____

_____

Social Goal:

_____

_____

_____

Spiritual Goal:

_____

_____

_____

Worksheet 10.1 Determining Goals & Objectives (Cont'd)

B. <u>Establishing Objectives</u>.

Objectives for Personal Goals:

_____

_____

_____

_____

_____

_____

Objectives for Professional Goals:

_____

_____

_____

_____

_____

_____

_____

_____

_____

_____

Worksheet 10.1 Determining Goals & Objectives (Cont'd)

Objectives for Social Goals:

_____

_____

_____

_____

_____

_____

_____

_____

Objectives for Spiritual Goals:

_____

_____

_____

_____

_____

_____

_____

_____

_____

_____

_____

Worksheet 10.2
Prioritizing Our Objectives

Let us now prioritize our objectives from all the four categories in the space provided below.

	More Important	**Less Important**
M o r e C h a n g e a b l e		
L e s s C h a n g e a b l e		

FEEDBACK ON WORKSHEET 10.2

Objectives relating to behavior changes that are more changeable and more important need to be our <u>first</u> priorities. Objectives which are more important and less changeable constitute our <u>second</u> priority. The <u>third</u> priority is objectives which are less important but more changeable. Less changeable and less important objectives need to be <u>ignored</u>.

* * * * * * * * * * * * * *

Worksheet 10.3
Deciding Targets

Having prioritized our objectives, we now need to make a daily list of targets which will help us accomplish the objectives selected. Since this is a daily activity, we can practice on a blank sheet of paper or make photocopies of this worksheet for repeated use.

Day & Date: _____

Time	Targets

Finding the Best Techniques that Suit Our Goals

All of us are different entities in ourselves. Our personalities, our biological constitution, our behaviors, our values, our attitudes, and our beliefs are unique. Likewise, our goals are also bound to be unique and personal. There may be a similarity of pattern in our attributes and goals with other individuals, but ultimately this set of attributes which each one of us has is totally unique and specific in itself. Therefore, as we have already seen, it is important to identify stress management and reduction techniques which suit this uniqueness in our individuality and our goals.

Worksheet 10.4 has been designed to provide us with an opportunity to identify and practice stress management and reduction techniques which suit our goals and "fit" our own unique individuality. These techniques, if practiced with <u>regularity</u> and <u>commitment</u> are bound to produce beneficial results in achieving our goals in life.

Thoughts for Reflection 10.3 helps us reinforce a sense of commitment with ourselves in order to keep up with the decided upon plan.

Thoughts for Reflection 10.3

Promise to Ourselves

Let us make a promise to ourselves, for our own good, that . . .

. . .   we shall make an effort to practice what we have learned.

. . .   we shall be disciplined and proactive in our approach.

. . .   we shall remain optimistic and positive about life.

. . .   we shall have faith in ourselves, our goals, and the techniques which we have learned.

. . .   we shall be enthusiastic and with zeal implement our plans.

. . .   we shall wear a cheerful countenance at all times and greet everyone around us with a smile.

. . .   we shall bless everyone around us, even if they may appear to be our enemies.

. . .   we shall devote all of our time for self-improvement so much so that we will have no time to find mistakes in others.

. . .   we shall have no unrealistic expectation from people and situations around us.

. . .   we shall try to understand more often than to be understood.

. . .   we shall be strong so much so that no worry over the future overpowers us or no past event disturbs our peace.

. . .   we shall be relaxed, happy, and contented in our disposition with our present.

* * * * * * * * * * * * * *

Worksheet 10.4
Stress Management and Reduction Techniques (SMART)
Practice Log

The SMART Practice Log has been designed to help learners experience and practice selected technique(s). We shall record the information in the SMART Practice Log for at least one week or until we have gained sufficient practice with the desired technique(s). The SMART Practice Log is an application tool.

What we need to do is to self rate the techniques which we practice in terms of their <u>effectiveness</u>, <u>ease of application</u>, and <u>practical utility</u>. We will, on a scale of 1 - 5, rate these criteria, that is: 1 = very low, 2 = low, 3 = satisfactory, 4 = high, and 5 = very high. We may want to use the terminology of not applicable (N/A) if we have not had enough opportunity to try the technique. Each technique has been provided with its respective worksheet number (W/S No.), for ready reference.

Techniques	W/S No.	Effective	Ease of Application	Practical Utility	Reasons
A. Relaxation Techniques					
Yogic Breathing or "Pranayama"	3.1				
Progressive Muscle Relaxation (PMR)	3.2				
Autogenic Training	3.3				
Visual Imagery	3.4				

Worksheet 10.4 Stress Management and Reduction Techniques (SMART) Practice Log (Cont'd)

Techniques	W/S No.	Effective	Ease of Application	Practical Utility	Reasons
B. Effective Communication					
Communication Assessment	4.1				
Situational Communication	4.2				
Assessing Assertive Behavior	4.3				
Becoming Assertive	4.4				
C. Anger Management					
Assessment	5.1				
Managing Our Anger	5.2				
Learning Active Listening	5.3				
D. Coping with Anxiety					
Assessment	6.1				
R.E.T	6.2				
SKY	6.3				

Worksheet 10.4 Stress Management and Reduction Techniques (SMART) Practice Log (Cont'd)

Techniques	W/S No.	Effective	Ease of Application	Practical Utility	Reasons
Gestalt Therapy	6.4				
Systematic Desensitization	6.5				
E. Balanced Diet and Appropriate Eating					
Awareness	7.1				
Plan	7.2				
F. Regular Exercise					
Awareness	8.1/ 8.2				
Exercise Program	8.3				
G. Time Management					
Awareness	9.1				
Practical Steps	9.2				
H. Goals & Objectives					
Determining	10.1				
Prioritizing	10.2				
Deciding Targets	10.3				

FEEDBACK ON WORKSHEET 10.4

This worksheet has provided us with insight into determining techniques which best suit our individuality in terms of effectiveness, ease of applicability, and practical utility. We have also discovered for ourselves the reasons for some of the techniques not being successful for us. If these reasons are under our control, then we can work at modifying them. However, if these reasons are not under our control, we need to find out and practice other techniques which work. The key for success lies in consistency and determination in our efforts in regularly practicing these techniques. These techniques are more helpful in preventing and reducing stress in comparison to managing stress. Therefore, the earlier is the age for starting and incorporating these techniques into our lives, the greater is the resultant benefit.

* * * * * * * * * * * * * *

Toward a Stress-Free Life

This Workbook has provided us with techniques for preventing, reducing, and managing stress in our lives. It is never too late to implement and practice these techniques regularly to obtain beneficial results. These results can be maximized if we incorporate these techniques within our daily life at a young age. Therefore, let us enter into an **Agreement** with ourselves to attain regularity in implementing the stress reduction plan in our lives. If we attain this regularity for a continuous period of at least one year, it will become fully etched within our system. In order to achieve this continuity, we may reward ourselves periodically with some tangible, self-decided rewards or incentives. Worksheet 10.5 has been designed to help us with this objective.

Another helpful way to ensure this regularity is through social networking or building social support. This social networking also contributes to managing our stress directly. We need to identify a close group of people around us who are available for listening empathically to our views and concerns, helping to clarify questions we have, and are willing to challenge us to grow if and when needed. Associating with such people is a boon and helps to prevent, reduce, and manage stress in our lives. Finally we would like to emphasize that by regularly practicing selected techniques identified through this workbook we can effectively manage our stress.

Worksheet 10.5
Self-Agreement

I, _____, hereby agree
to practice selected techniques for stress management identified as beneficial
and practical for me from the SMART Practice Log. I shall not procrastinate
any further the implementation of these techniques in my life. I shall
observe utmost regularity and a sense of discipline in implementing these
techniques.

I shall periodically reward myself for this accomplishment. After attaining regularity for . . .

1 month: I shall _____
                                          (reward)

_____

3 months: I shall _____
                                          (reward)

_____

6 months: I shall _____
                                          (reward)

_____

1 year: I shall _____
                                          (reward)

_____

* * * * * * * * * * * * * *

Stress Management Principle # 10

Let us work on a plan, then the plan will work on us.

Summary Points

- Implementation of a plan is central for success.

- Self motivation and degree of changeability are prerequisites for implementing a plan.

- The behaviors which are more important and more changeable deserve our first priority in implementation.

- We need to take stock of all our resources before we implement a plan. This includes soliciting help from other people close to us and obtaining necessary material resources.

- Goals are an indication of what we want to accomplish in our life. They cover four different spheres of life, namely personal, professional, social, and spiritual.

- Goal analysis or goal setting is a procedure useful in helping us describe the meaning of what we want to achieve in terms of attitude and understanding.

- Maslow's Hierarchy of Needs Theory on Motivation identifies five levels of needs viz. physiological, security, love, self-esteem, and self-actualization.

- Alderfer's ERG Theory describes the core needs of existence, relatedness, and growth.

- Objectives can be defined as concerted, directed, focused, stepwise efforts at achieving goals.

- Some attributes of objectives include precision, determined time frame, realistic, sequenced, proactive, preferably written, measurable, and behaviorally oriented.

- Deciding targets includes planning for the various day to day activities required in accomplishing goals and objectives.

- According to Eastern philosophy success of any result is dependent upon effort, direction, and an unknown factor.

- Regular practice of techniques described in this workbook will help us in preventing, reducing, and managing our stress.

References and Further Readings

Alderfer, C. (1969, May). An empirical test of a new theory of human needs. Organizational Behavioral and Human Performance, 142-175.

Addington, J. E. (1977). All about goals and how to achieve them. Marina del Rey, CA: DeVorss & Company.

Green, L. G., & Kreuter, M. W. (1991). Health promotion planning. An educational and environmental approach (2nd ed.). Mountain View, CA: Mayfield Publishing Company.

Liebler, J. G., Levine, R. E., & Rothman, J. (1992). Management principles for health professionals (2nd ed.). Gaithersburg, MD: Aspen Publishers, Inc.

Mager, R. F. (1972). Goal analysis. Belmont, CA: Fearon Publishers/Lear Siegler, Inc.

Maslow, A. (1954). Motivation and personality. New York, NY: Harper and Row Publishers.

Maslow, A. (1962). Toward a psychology of being. Monterey, CA: Brooks/Cole Publishing Company.

Robbins, S.P. (1989). Organizational behavior. Concepts, controversies, and applications. (4th ed.). Englewood Cliffs, NJ: Prentice Hall, Inc.

LIST OF STRESS MANAGEMENT PRINCIPLES

1   It is not the stressor but the perception of the stress by us which is important.

2   We need to become aware before considering change.

3   Let us make relaxation a part of life.

4   We need to think first before passing judgement.

5   Balancing our anger balances our life.

6   We need to wipe out anxiety before it wipes us out.

7   Enjoy balanced meals at regular times and cherish the gift.

8   Let us start an exercise program and keep exercising regularly.

9   Do it now!

#10   Let us work on a plan, then the plan will work on us.

* * * * * * * * * * * * *

J.A.R.
M.S.

Guide to Pronunciation of Foreign Language Words

Abhnivesha, 17 əbh – nē'– vāsh

Adhi, 17, 29 ä'– dē

Adhibhotik, 17, 18 ädhi – bhô – tik

Adhidevik, 17, 18 ädhi – de – vik

Adhyatmik, 17, 18 ädhyät'– mik

Agna Chakra, 70 ägna – chäk'– rä

Ahankara, 16, 29 əhn'– kärə

Ananda, 64 ä – nända

Asaana, 69 äsana

Asmita, 17 əs – mitä'

Asthangayoga, 69 ästhan – yoog

Atharva, 16 əth'– ərv

Atman, 16, 29 ätmə

Avidya, 17, 29 ä – vid'– yä

Ayurvedic, 16 ä – yoor – vā'– dəc

Bhagvad Gita, 16 bhəg – vəth' gētä

Bhakti Yoga, 69 bhäktē – yoog

Brahma Sutras, 16 brähm – sōo'– tra

Chakra Yoga, 69 chäk'– rä yoog

Chakras, 69 chäk'– räs

Charaka Samhita, 16 chə – rəkə sə – nhitä'

Dharana, 69 dhər – ənə

Dhyana, 69 dhy – ənə

Dukha, 16, 29 doo – khə'

Dvesha, 17 dvāsh

Estresse, 10 es – tress – ē

Gyana, 17 gyä – nə

   Yoga, 69 yoog

Hatha Yoga, 69 hath – ä yoog

Kama, 16, 23, 29 käm

Karma Yoga, 69 kər'– mə yoog

Kaya Kalpa, 71 kə – yä kal – pa

Klesa, 16, 29 kĺa – shə

Kriya Yoga, 70-71, 94 krī – yä yoog

Kumbhaka, 71 kumb – haka

Kundalini Shakti, 69-70, 94
        kun – da – lēnē shə – ktē'

Lobh, 23 lôbh

Madh, 17 mədh

Moh, 23 mōoh

Mooladhara, 70 mool – əd – hərə

Mudra Yoga, 69 mōo – drə yoog

Niyama, 69 n̄i – yäm

Prajanaparadha, 17 prə – jən – pərədə'

Pranayama, 69, 71-72, 75-77, 94, 269 pränä - yäm

Pratihara, 69 prät – i – hərə

Prosupta, 16, 23 prō – sōoptə

Puraka, 71 pur – əkə'

Puranas, 16 poo – rän

Raja Yoga, 69 rəjə yoog

Rechaka, 71 rec – həkə

Relaxare, 67 re – lax – āre

Rig, 16 rigg

Sahasrara, 69, 70 səh – əs – rar

Sama, 16 säm

Samadhi, 69 sä – mädhi

    Bhavna, 17 bhəv – nə

Samkhya-yoga, 17 sän – khy yoog

Shanti Yoga, 70 shrē – ti yoog

Srimad Bhagvatam, 17 shrē'– məd bhä –
vətəm'

Stresse, 10 stress – ē

Strictus, 10 stric – tus

Susruta Samhita, 16 sōosh – rōothä sə – nhitä'

Tantaras, 16 tənt'– ra

Tonu, 17, 23 tô – nōo

Trisna, 22 trē – shnä'

Udara, 16, 23 ōo – dər

Upanishads, 16 upä – ni – shads

Veda(s), 16, 69 vā'– das

    Atharva, 16 əth'– ərv

    Rig, 16 rigg

    Sama, 16 säm

    Yajur, 16 yə'– jōor

Vichchinna, 17, 23 vi – chinə

Vidya, 17 vid'– yä

Yajur, 16 yə'– jōor

Yama, 69 yäm

Yoga, 69, 94 yoog

    Asthanga, 69 ästhan

    Bhakti, 69 bhäktē

    Chakra, 69 chäk'– rä

    Gyana, 69 gyä – nə

    Hatha, 69 hath – ä

    Karma, 69 kər'– mə

    Kriya, 69, 70-71, 94 krī yä

    Mudra, 69 mōo – drə

    Raja, 69 rəjə

Yogasutras, 16, 69 yoog – sōo – trä

PRONUNCIATION KEY

Symbol	Key Words		Symbol	Key Words
a	asp, fat, parrot		b	bed, fable, dub, ebb
ā	ape, date, play, break, fail		d	dip, beadle, had, dodder
ä	ah, car, father, cot		f	fall, after, off, phone
			g	get, haggle, dog
e	elf, ten, berry		h	he, ahead, hotel
ē	even, meet, money, flea, grief		j	joy, agile, badge
			k	kill, tackle, bake, coat, quick
i	is, hit, mirror		l	let, yellow, ball
ī	ice, bite, high, sky		m	met, camel, trim, summer
			n	not, flannel, ton
ō	open, tone, go, boat		p	put, apple, tap
ô	all, horn, law, oar		r	red, port, dear, purr
oo	look, pull, moor, wolf		s	sell, castle, pass, nice
o͞o	ooze, tool, crew, rule		t	top, cattle, hat
yo͞o	use, cute, few		v	vat, hovel, have
yoo	cure, globule		w	will, always, swear, quick
oi	oil, point, toy		y	yet, onion, yard
ou	out, crowd, plow		z	zebra, dazzle, haze, rise
u	up, cut, color, flood		ch	chin, catcher, arch, nature
ʉr	urn, fur, deter, irk		sh	she, cushion, dash, machine
			th	thin, nothing, truth
ə	a in ago		*th*	then, father, lathe
	e in agent		zh	azure, leisure, beige
	i in sanity		ŋ	ring, anger, drink
	o in comply		'	[indicates that a following l
	u in focus			or n is a syllabic consonant,
ər	perhaps, murder			as in *cattle* (kat''l), *Latin*
				(lat''n)

FOREIGN SOUNDS

à This symbol, representing the *a* in French *salle*, can best be described as intermediate between (a) and (ä).

ë This symbol represents the sound of the vowel cluster in French *coeur* and can be approximated by rounding the lips as for (ō) and pronouncing (e).

ö This symbol variously represents the sound of *eu* in French *feu* or of *ö* or *oe* in German *blöd* or *Goethe* and can be approximated by rounding the lips as for (ō) and pronouncing (ā).

ô̂ This symbol represents a range of sounds between (ô) and (u); it occurs typically in the sound of the *o* in French *tonne* or German *korrekt*; in Italian *poco* and Spanish *torero*, it is almost like English (ô), as in *horn*.

ü This symbol variously represents the sound of *u* in French *duc* and in German *grün* and can be approximated by rounding the lips as for (ō) and pronouncing (ē).

kh This symbol represents the voiceless velar or uvular fricative as in the *ch* of German *doch* or Scots English *loch*. It can be approximated by placking the tongue as for (k) but allowing the breath to escape in a stream, as in pronouncing (h).

H This symbol represents a sound similar to the preceding but formed by friction against the forward part of the palate, as in German *ich*. It can be made by placing the tongue as for English (sh) but with the tip pointing downward.

n This symbol indicates that the vowel sound immediately preceding it is nasalized; that is, the nasal passage is left open so that the breath passes through both the mouth and the nose in voicing the vowel, as in French *mon* (mōn). The letter *n* itself is not pronounced unless followed by a vowel.

r This symbol represents any of various sounds used in languages other than English for the consonant *r*. It may represent the tongue-point trill or uvular trill of the *r* in French *reste* or *sur*, German *Reuter*, Italian *ricotta*, Russian *gorod*, etc.

' The apostrophe is used after final *l* and *r*, in certain French pronunciations, to indicate that they are voiceless after an unvoiced consonant, as in *lettre* (let'r'). In Russian words the "soft sign" in the Cyrillic spelling is indicated by (y'). The sound can be approximated by pronouncing an unvoiced (y) directly after the consonant involved, as in *Sevastopol* (se' väs tô' pəl y').

Index